OXFORD MEDICAL PUBLICATIONS

Terminal Care at Home

OXFORD GENERAL PRACTICE SERIES

Editorial Board

G. H. FOWLER, J. A. M. GRAY,
J. C. HASLER, D. C. MORRELL,
A.-L. KINMONTH

1. Paediatric problems in general practice
   M. Modell and R. H. Boyd
2. Geriatric problems in general practice
   G. Wilcock, J. A. M. Gray, and P. M. M. Pritchard
3. Preventive medicine in general practice
   edited by J. A. M. Gray and G. H. Fowler
4. Women's problems in general practice
   edited by A. McPherson and A. Anderson
5. Locomotor disability in general practice
   edited by M. I. V. Jayson and R. Million
6. The consultation: an approach to learning and teaching
   D. Pendleton, T. Schofield, P. Tate, and P. Havelock
7. Continuing care: the management of chronic disease
   edited by J. C. Hasler and T. P. C. Schofield
8. Management in general practice
   P. M. M. Pritchard, K. B. Low, and M. Whalen
9. Modern obstetrics in general practice
   edited by G. N. Marsh
10. Terminal care at home
    edited by Roy Spilling

Terminal Care at Home

Oxford General Practice Series 10

Edited by

ROY SPILLING
General Practitioner, Oxford

OXFORD   NEW YORK   TOKYO
OXFORD UNIVERSITY PRESS
1986

Oxford University Press, Walton Street, Oxford OX2 6DP
Oxford New York Toronto
Delhi Bombay Calcutta Madras Karachi
Kuala Lumpur Singapore Hong Kong Tokyo
Nairobi Dar es Salaam Cape Town
Melbourne Auckland
and associated companies in
Beirut Berlin Ibadan Nicosia

Oxford is a trade mark of Oxford University Press

Published in the United States
by Oxford University Press, New York

© Roy Spilling, 1986

All rights reserved. No part of this publication may be reproduced,
stored in a retrieval system, or transmitted, in any form or by any means,
electronic, mechanical, photocopying, recording, or otherwise, without
the prior permission of Oxford University Press.

This book is sold subject to the condition that it shall not, by way
of trade or otherwise, be lent, re-sold, hired out or otherwise circulated
without the publisher's prior consent in any form of binding or cover
other than that in which it is published and without a similar condition
including this condition being imposed on the subsequent purchaser

British Library Cataloguing in Publication Data
Terminal care at home.—(Oxford general practice
series; 10)
1. Terminal care 2. Home care services
I. Spilling, Roy
362.14   R726.8
ISBN 0-19-261508-4

Library of Congress Cataloging in Publication Data
Main entry under title:
Terminal care at home.
(Oxford general practice series; 10)
Includes bibliographies and index.
1. Terminally ill—Home care. 2. Terminal care.
3. Cancer—Patients—Home care. 4. Home care
services—Great Britain. I. Spilling, Roy. II. Series:
Oxford general practice series; no. 10. [DNLM:
1. Home Care Services. 2. Hospices. 3. Terminal
Care. W1 OX55 no. 10/WB 310 T3192]
R726.8.T464   1986   649'.8   85-25887
ISBN 0-19-261508-4 (pbk.)

Set by Spire Print Services Ltd, Salisbury, Wilts
Printed in Great Britain by St Edmundsbury Press,
Bury St Edmunds, Suffolk

Preface

Deaths at home are caused by many different pathological processes and tabulated in different diagnostic groupings. Of these, the commonest cause of death in the UK is a disorder of circulation (see Table. 1.1). Despite being less common, in the field of terminal care, malignant disease assumes greater importance as some degree of preparation for death is possible. Respiratory disease, while causing death nearly as often, does not create such public alarm as cancer. Because of the widespread fear, and the one in five risk of dying from a malignancy, most of this book deals with terminal care in the context of a diagnosis of cancer.

For the population at large, the word cancer arouses a set of closely related fears: a lingering death, intolerable pain, inevitable helplessness. The medical profession has responded to this reaction by avoiding direct references to cancer, at least within earshot of the patient. Yet the progression of symptoms convinces the dying of the truth of their plight. Failure to discuss what these symptoms mean increases the patient's fear and isolation. The stereotyping of relationships which occurs in institutions allows both staff and relatives of patients dying in hospital to maintain a conspiracy of silence longer than if they die at home. But the family at home cannot hide behind institutional walls. The general practitioner, too, aims to respond openly to his patient whom he has known through good times and bad. Great demands are therefore placed on those entering general practice whose training has largely been in a hospital environment. This book is written with the young general practitioner in mind. Chapters on 'Dying at home' and 'Communication' aim to bridge the gap from the hospital context to the community.

Symptoms can be as well controlled at home as in hospital, but the practitioner will need to know the particular skills of his practice team, especially of the community nursing sister. He may need to draw on the extra support of specialist nurses in terminal care. The hospice movement has pioneered many new services, and insights provided both from the care of adults and children can be adopted by those working in the community. To a technological world which has slipped the theological moorings of a former generation, the special perspective of the clergy can restore some of the normality and significance of death and grief. The aim of this book is to enable both the strong and the weak, those giving and those receiving, to live while dying.

Oxford R.S.
September, 1985

Acknowledgements

The author would like to acknowledge the following sources of quotations and illustrations:

The quotations on p. xi and p. 147 are from 'Little Gidding' in *Four Quartets*, reproduced with permission of Faber and Faber and Harcourt Brace Jovanovich. The quotation on p. 92 is reprinted by permission of the publishers and the Trustees of Amherst College from *The poems of Emily Dickinson*, edited by Thomas H. Johnson, Cambridge Mass.: Reprinted by permission of Little, Brown, and Company and The Belknap Press of Harvard University Press, copyright 1951 © 1955, 1979, 1983, by the President and Fellows of Harvard College. Table 8.1 on p. 140 is from *Letting go* by Ainsworth-Smith and Speck, reproduced with permission of SPCK, The Society for Promoting Christian Knowledge. Figure 3.2 on p. 39 and Table 3.2 on p. 40 are reproduced with permission of Professor Patrick Wall, Editor of *Pain*. Figure 5.1 on p. 84 is reproduced with permission of Academic Press Inc. Some of the material in Chapter 7 by Mother Frances Dominica has been published in *Hospice approaches to paediatric care* (ed. Professor Charles A. Corr and Donna M. Corr), Springer Publishing Co, New York (1985), and is used with permission. The quotations of Rabindranath Tagore on p. 1 and p. 17 are used with permission of Macmillan Publishing Company.

Contents

List of contributors		x
1	**Dying at home**	1
	Roy Spilling	
	Reasons for hospital admission in terminal illness	2
	Understanding prevailing trends	4
	The contemporary scene	6
	Reactions to the contemporary scene	7
	Home care provision	11
	The role of the general practitioner	13
	The general practitioner's training	16
	Conclusion	16
2	**The development of home care services in the UK**	19
	Prue Clench	
	The demand	19
	Types and trends in community services	20
	The development of the Dorothy House Foundation	21
	How do teams function in relation to the primary care team?	27
	What do teams offer the general practitioner?	30
	Establishing home care teams	33
3	**Symptom control**	35
	Robert Twycross	
	General considerations	36
	Pain control	38
	Use of analgesics	43
	Nausea and vomiting	49
	Obstruction	50
	Anorexia	52
	'Squashed stomach syndrome'	53
	Obstructive lymphoedema	54
	Use of corticosteroids	56
	Confusion about confusion	57
	Confusional states	58
4	**Nursing care at home**	64
	Alison Charles–Edwards	
	General philosophy of care	64
	The patient as an individual	64

viii *Contents*

	Emotional support	63
	Physical aspects of nursing care	65
	Care of relatives and close friends	74
	Practicalities	78
	Conclusion	82
5	**Communication**	**83**
	Roy Spilling	
	Introduction	83
	The consultation	84
	The dying process	86
	Problems of communicating with the dying	89
	Communication within families	93
	Some practical conclusions	94
6	**Hospice care**	**96**
	Robert Twycross	
	What is hospice care?	96
	Variations on a theme	97
	Evaluation of hospice care	99
	Appropriate treatment	100
	Rehabilitation	104
	Hope	105
	Professional friendship	106
	Care of the whole person	106
	Team-work	108
	Are hospices really necessary?	109
	Conclusion	110
7	**The dying child: a hospice for children**	**113**
	Frances Dominica	
	Introduction	113
	Helen	113
	The building	115
	The team	117
	Liaison with other agencies and families	118
	'Hospice' and 'terminal illness'	119
	The selection of children	120
	Pattern of visits	121
	Referrals	122
	Case histories	122
	The child and his family	125
	Practical care of the child	129
	Conclusion	129

8	**The care of the family in dying and grieving: a pastoral approach**	131
	David Atkinson	
	Introduction	131
	What is pastoral care?	132
	A theological approach to dying and grieving	134
	Coping with grief	137
	The place of ritual in grieving	143
	Loss and growth	145
Index		**149**

Contributors

David Atkinson, B.Sc., Ph.D., M.Litt
Chaplain and Fellow of Corpus Christi College, Oxford

Alison Charles–Edwards, SRN, H.V. Cert.
Former Ward Sister, Sir Michael Sobell House, Oxford

Prue Clench, MBE, SRN
Nurse Adviser on Terminal Care Services, London

Frances Dominica, RSCN, FRCN
Mother Superior, All Saints Convent, Oxford

Roy Spilling, MA, MRCGP
General Practitioner, Oxford

Robert Twycross, MA, DM, FRCP
Consultant Physician, Sir Michael Sobell House, Oxford

What we call the beginning is often the end
And to make an end is to make a beginning.
The end is where we start from.

> T. S. Eliot
> From *Four Quartets*

1 Dying at home

Roy Spilling

My house is small and what once has gone from it can never be regained.
Rabindranath Tagore
Gitanjali

There are many reasons why most people, if given the option, would choose to die at home. That preference is expressed both by those dying in hospital, (Rossman and Kissick 1961) and by reports of those dying at home (Aitken-Swan 1959). Home is where most people feel secure; the scene is familiar, collected objects symbolize significant events, and important people—husband, wife, parent, child—are near to hand. If separated by distance or death, these relationships are remembered by photographs, furniture, wallpaper, and in many other less tangible ways. Home is where we have chosen to live, and the surroundings of our home will encourage us to live while dying.

Apart from providing security, home also represents freedom; to eat when and what one wishes, sleep when necessary, choose one's company. Many other freedoms have already been lost by the terminally ill patient; freedom to work, indulge in sport, or even just walk the dog. A ward routine will add to this loss of freedom and increase a sense of dependence.

Hospital admission may, however, be necessary to provide adequate care. The decision to move a terminally ill patient from home should be taken in the knowledge that, in addition to loss of familiarity and freedom, an element of hope will be also lost. Most dying patients know of their predicament (Saunders 1959), and their move from home will be for many, the final nail in their coffin. Professor Wilkes found that 25 per cent of his admissions to St. Luke's, Sheffield, died in less than three days (Wilkes 1980*a*). The shortening of life span has already been shown to be an effect of moving long-stage geriatric patients from one situation to another.

Despite these real advantages of choosing to stay at home, statistics confirm that approximately two-thirds of deaths take place in institutions and only one-third at home (Hughes 1960; Cartwright *et al.* 1973). The causes of death will determine, to some extent, the place of death (Table 1.1), but even in malignant disease, when death tends to be expected, the recent trend confirms a reduction of deaths at home (Table 1.2).

2 Dying at home

Table 1.1. Place and cause of death in England and Wales, 1969

Diagnostic groups	Pecentage of total deaths (579 378)	Percentage in each group dying in:	
		Hospital	Home
Circulatory	52	52	48
Neoplastic	20	63	37
Respiratory	15	65	35
Accidents	4	53	47
Other	9	80	20

After Cartwright *et al.* (1973).

Table 1.2. Deaths at home as percentages of all, and of cancer deaths

Year	All deaths	At home (%)	Cancer deaths	At home (%)
1965	549 000	38	107 000	37
1974	585 000	31	123 000	31
1983	580 000	32	134 000	32

Figures obtained from the Registrar General's Statistical Review of England and Wales (1976 and 1984) and rounded off to the nearest thousand.

REASONS FOR HOSPITAL ADMISSIONS IN TERMINAL ILLNESS

It is easy to find reasons for this trend.

1. Hospitals are able to offer continuous nursing care for those who need much physical help.
2. Some techniques of pain relief, such as local radiotherapy, or neuro-surgical blocks, are available only in hospitals.
3. The family doctor may feel that his specialist colleagues have more to offer, particularly if there are symptoms which defy his diagnostic skill.
4. The increasing proportion of elderly in our population will stretch the community and neighbourly care services (Table 1.3).
5. An increased percentage of the elderly now live alone (Table 1.4).
6. Those with whom the elderly do live (Table 1.5), are likely themselves to be older, and less able to care for a dying relative or friend. Fifteen per cent of those dying at home were cared for by relatives over 70 years of age (Cartwright *et al.* 1973).
7. The increased mobility of the population has reduced the likelihood of children living nearby. The Age Concern Survey (1974) shows

Table 1.3. The elderly population of the UK (thousands)

	1951	1971	1975
Men			
65–74	1600	2000	2161
75+	700	800	871
Total	2300	2800	3032
Women			
60–74	3500	4500	4592
75+	1100	1800	1911
Total	4600	6300	6483
All over retirement age as percentage of total population	13.6	16.3	17.0

From Central Statistical Office 1976 Social Trends No. 7. HMSO, London.

Table 1.4. The elderly population living alone in private households in the UK (percentages)

	1951	1971
Men (%)		
65–74	6.5	10.9
75+	10.5	17.7
All elderly men (%)	7.7	13.0
Women (%)		
60–74	15.6	27.0
75+	23.1	37.5
All elderly women (%)	16.8	30.0

From Central Statistical office 1973 Social Trends No. 4. HMSO, London.

Table 1.5. Who do the elderly live with? UK 1973–74 (percentages)

Spouse	41
Married children	7
Umarried daughter	5
Unmarried son	7
Grandchildren	4
Other relatives (65 or over)	4
Other relatives (65 or under)	3
Non-relatives	3
Alone	26

From Age Concern (1974).

that 40 per cent of the elderly did not have children living within one hour's distance. Even those who had children seemed worried about imposing on them.
8. More of the wives of married children had full- or part-time employment.
9. It is also less common to find unmarried children with the time or suitable accommodation to nurse an elderly relative.
10. Public expectation of hospital as the appropriate place to die has increased over the years in our Western culture.

UNDERSTANDING PREVAILING TRENDS

Insights from history

Contemporary trends are best understood in their historical context by considering the contribution made from other disciplines.

Archaeology has evidence of funerary customs very early in man's history. In the Shanidar cave in northern Iraq, Dr Ralph Solecki found a Neanderthal skull (approximately 60 000 BC) surrounded by mammalian bones, evidence of fire, and eight species of flowers woven into branches of a shrub (quoted by Jonas in Toynbee 1968). Another skull of a similar age, found in a hollow of a cave floor at La Chapelle-aux-Saints in south-west France, had the bone and flesh of a bison adjacent to it. This assumed requirement of the dead for sustenance is further demonstrated by the discovery of food and drink in Bronze Age barrows (Hawkes 1952). In certain respects, early man indicated a need to keep the dead alive; but these burial finds were well apart from remains of everyday life. The further necessity, in some cultures, for living wives or servants of the dead chief, to be buried alive with him (Durkheim 1897) implies that there should be no reason for the dead to return and haunt the living. In some senses, then, funerary customs can be interpreted as seeking to keep the dead alive, but apart from the living.

Social historians such as Philippe Ariès bring us up to date with more contemporary observations from a study of graveyards and gravestones (Ariès 1976). In his masterly essay tracing Western attitudes from the Middle Ages to the present day, he begins with the eleventh-century age of chivalry. The Christian knight was not only forewarned of death by natural signs or inward conviction, but he also prepared for his end in a ritual way. This involved the expression of sorrow, the pardoning of his companions, and then the prayer of confession, commitment, and absolution. He presided over his own death which was expected to be a public occasion. This peaceful acceptance of the dead and dying by the living characterized the eleventh-century view, which Ariès calls 'tamed death'. By the nineteenth-century, through the influence of the Romantic

Movement, death had become glorified with ostentation and sentimentality which would have a reaction in the twentieth-century 'forbidden death'.

Insights from animal behaviour

This 'forbidding' of death, or thoughts of death, is our particular culture's way of dealing with the fear of dying. The fear itself can be shown to have survival value, as researchers in animal behaviour have demonstrated. Workers such as Lorenz, Tinbergen, and Dawkins, have helped the understanding of human grief and fear of death. Lorenz (1963), for example, describes the searching behaviour of a separated Greylag goose from its mate.

The first response to the disappearance of the partner consists in the anxious attempt to find him again. The goose moves about restlessly by day and night, flying great distances and visiting places where the partner might be found, uttering all the time the penetrating trisyllabic long-distance call. . . . All the objective observable characteristics of the goose's behaviour on losing its mate are roughly identical with human grief.

Such behaviour can readily be understood as having survival value, the calling and searching making it more likely that the lost partner is found. Similar behaviour has been reported of children aged between 15 and 30 months, on admission to institutional care (Robertson 1953).

In this initial phase, which may last from a few hours to 7 or 8 days, the young child has a strong conscious need of his mother and the expectation, based on previous experience that she will respond to his cries . . . he will often cry loudly, shake his cot, throw himself about and look eagerly towards any sight or sound which may prove to be his missing mother.

This behaviour is an expression of emotion, sometimes described as separation anxiety, or more generally, fear. Fear of death includes fear of separation as one of its foci (see Table 5.2, p. 87). Similar fear is felt in conditions associated with danger—noise, strangeness, rapid approach, darkness—so that Bowlby (1975) concludes

. . . the young of species that have survived, including man, are found to be genetically biased so as to develop that they respond to the properties of noise, strangeness, sudden approach, and darkness by taking avoiding action or running away—they behave in fact as though danger were actually present. In a comparable way they respond to isolation by seeking company. Fear responses elicited by such naturally occurring clues to danger are a part of man's basic behaviour and equipment.

Considered in this light, man's fear of death has survival value. If this factor is relevant, then fear of death after successful rearing of a family would be expected to recede—a finding confirmed by Munnichs' (1966) study of

6   *Dying at home*

100 Dutch elders: 'Only a small category of old people were in fear of the end.' Conversely, death of those with family responsibilities or of children denied the possibility of procreation, would be expected to be particularly poignant.

THE CONTEMPORARY SCENE

Several different factors conspire to 'forbid' death in our own culture.

1. The attempt to hide the truth from the dying by the living; argued both for their own sake, and also for the sake of society. Expressions of distress or despair are painful for the living to witness.
2. The improved technology available to doctors has resulted in a change of public perception, so that they, rather than the clergy, are appropriate presidents over the dying process. This has coincided with a falling off of public religious practice.
3. Improved public health and scientific medicine have increased public expectation of longevity; so that doctors even in the terminal care field have been invested by the dying with hope of cure.
4. Our contemporary medical school training, with its emphasis on high technology curative medicine, ill equips most graduates with skills for maintaining hope while bodily function degenerates. This professional denial further 'forbids' death.
5. Improved infant mortality and increased longevity have made the experience of caring for the dying more unusual in our culture than it was 50 years ago. This has been accentuated by the increased tendency for death to take place in hospital.
6. Decreased awareness of the dying process tends to increase anxiety with fantasy at the expense of fact.

Technology and institutions

These and other factors have removed dying from the thoroughfare of life into institutions which more often than not take the shape of general hospitals. This medicalization of death, Illich (1976) argues, increases the dependence which living communities have of high technology medicine. 'The dominant image of death determines the prevalent concept of health' (p. 179), and that for our generation, the concept of 'Natural death is the history of the medicalisation of the struggle against death' (p. 181), 'Within an industrial society, medical intervention in everyday life does not change the prevailing image of health and death, but rather caters to it' producing a society in which 'consumers religiously prepare themselves for hospital deaths' (p. 207). 'Natural death' has become a technical one.

Illustrating this from the American experience, Kastenbaum and Aisenberg (1972) write:

even within hospital walls, there are implicit rules and choices. The hospitalised patient is not supposed to die in just any place at any time. It is deemed important that he does not expose the survivors (other patients, staff, visitors) to the phenomenon of death except under carefully specified circumstances. The obliging terminal patient will first provide clear evidence, either through clinical symptoms or laboratory findings, to the effect that his condition is worsening. This enables the medico-administrative process to add his name to the danger list. He will then show clear signs of further deterioration or jeopardy which require either that special treatments begin on his present ward, or preferably, that he be transferred to an intensive treatment unit. Here he will eventually provide indices of impending death. Now he may be removed to a private side-room. Death is expected. The approach sequence is winding to its finale. The chaplain and other non-medical constituents of the system can enact their roles in the customary manner.

The wheel has turned full circle; we can in effect do what Stone Age man ritually symbolized in his burial customs. Our technology enables us to keep the dead alive, and our hospital institutions allow us to remove them from the living.

REACTIONS TO THE CONTEMPORARY SCENE

Technology and institutions, these two characteristics of modern medicine, seem, in many instances, inappropriate to the care of the dying patient. Patients also, as consumers, are able to make their feelings known, as Goffman (1961) illustrates in *Asylums*. He argues that patients take themselves for repair to the medical profession as broken machines are taken to workshops. He points out:

the body is one possession that cannot be left under the care of the server while the client goes about his other business. Admittedly, physicians show a remarkable capacity to carry on the verbal part of the server role while engaging in the mechanical part, without the segregation breaking down, but there are inevitable difficulties here, since the client is very interested in what is happening to his body and is in a good position to see what is being done. One solution is anaesthesia; another is the wonderful brand of 'non-person treatment' found in the medical world, whereby the patient is greeted with what passes as civility, and said farewell to in the same fashion, with everything in between going on as if the patient were not there as a social person at all, only as a possession someone has left behind.

The hospice movement

Sensitive doctors working in the field of terminal care have been responsive to the perceived and expressed needs of patients and their families. It was in response to the request of a dying patient that Dame Cicely Saunders pioneered St. Christopher's Hospice, London which has provided the pattern for many other hospice units. The first £500 towards the hospice came from a refugee from Poland who died in 1948 in a busy surgical ward. This patient, David Tasma, said to Dame Cicely: 'I want what is in your mind and in your heart . . . I want to be a window in your home' (Stoddart 1979). Robert Twycross in Chapter 6 of this book, illustrates the role which hospices can play in the care of the dying. Faced with a terminally ill child, some parents expressed the need for a support unit to enable them to cope with keeping their child at home. In response to this request, Helen House in Oxford was planned and opened in November 1982, and the analysis of the first year is reported by Byrne *et al.* (1984). The concept of hospice-assisted home care of children is expanded by Mother Frances Dominica in Chapter 7 of this book. However, severely ill children need to be discharged from hospital if they are to die at home. This requires courage and faith from the parents and hospital staff alike (Cotton and Goodall 1981).

Patient participation groups

It is possible to obtain the opinions of patients without waiting for them to be expressed. Peter Pritchard (1975) has described the way a patient participation group can be inaugurated, and gives an account of it in practice. Community health councils could co-operate, and the Royal College of General Practitioners has supported the development of patient participation groups (RCGP 1981). The requirements of the terminally ill and the planning of services to meet these may be well perceived by other key members of the local community. A parish vicar, for example, may find himself in a special position to assess the needs of the dying and bereaved.

Comparisons with the home birth movement

If we listen to the voice of the consumer challenging the relevance of technology and institutions to natural events, still more consideration will have to be given to dying at home. At the beginning and end of life, the movements for 'natural childbirth' and 'natural death' see the home as the appropriate setting for these signficant events. One reason against domiciliary birth, the risk to the baby, has no counterpart in the case against dying at home. However, some arguments for birth at home find strong agreement with those for dying at home Sagov (1984) lists:

1. control of the process remaining with the patient and his family,
2. being able to relax and feeling secure as essential ingredients of the process,
3. being able to choose those present,
4. therefore seeking only supportive attendance,
5. requiring justification for any intervention,
6. avoiding separation from family and friends,
7. feeling alienated in hospital as opposed to remaining at home.

Bereavement care

A further reaction to the denial of death and ignoring of grief, widespread in the first half of the twentieth century, has been an increased interest in bereavement. In the United Kingdom, Colin Murray Parkes has pioneered our understanding of abnormal and normal grief, and his excellent book *Bereavement*, first published in 1972, and now a Penguin paperback, has provided a scholarly readable introduction to the subject.

The behaviour associated with grief will be influenced by the processes occurring during bereavement. The attempt to avoid or deny the loss, the need to search for the dead person, and the gradual acceptance of the absence of the loved one, will wax and wane in their pre-eminence as time progresses. The pattern for each person will vary, but it is important to have a picture of normal grief. Although simplified, the following table is offered as an *aide-mémoire*.

Some of the symptoms associated with grief may, of course be experienced before the moment of death. The diagnosis of inoperable cancer, or of irretrievable brain damage following an accident, may initiate the grief process.

Resolution of grief is associated with the establishing of a new identity, incorporating the loss, but managing to form again new relationships. This may not happen in the first two years, although for many, it progresses through a series of achievements beginning after the first few months Such tasks might include:

Dealing with the un-needed clothes
 – Rearranging the bedroom
 – Revisiting significant places
 – Entertaining friends

If the death has taken place in hospital, revisiting the ward and talking to the staff can be a major hurdle to overcome.

Armed with an understanding of normal grief, the general practitioner will seek to spot departures from the norm. He may be aware of risk factors, such as previous psychiatric illness in the surviving spouse, or an ambivalent or over-dependent relationship with the dead person. Undue delay in onset of the pangs of grief beyond the first two weeks, increased intensity of guilt, and development of identification symptoms, suggest that grief might be pursuing a pathological course. Such pathological grief reactions are usually more prolonged, symptoms often being experienced well beyond two years. Specific thoughts of suicide, as opposed to wishing not to be alive, should lead to psychiatric intervention. It is more difficult to decide whether or not to treat symptoms of normal grief such as insomnia or anxiety. Although there is little available data, it could be argued that preventing the symptoms of normal grief might simply be delaying their resolution. Hypnotics and tranquillizers, the most commonly

Table 1.6.

Phase	Characteristics	Onset	Duration
Shock	Numbness Panic	From confirmation of death	Up to two weeks
Early 'yearning' phase	(a) Pangs—the experience of severe anxiety and psychological pain associated with 'fight or flight' sympathetic activity	Usually within a few hours of bereavement	Maximal in second week Usually recede by six weeks Occur after that with reminders

	(b) Searching—goal-directed behaviour
	  1. State of arousal
	  2. Restless movement
	  3. Preoccupation with thoughts of the deceased
	  4. Development of perceptual set for him/her
	  5. Loss of interest in personal appearance
	  6. Direction of attention to environment where the lost person is likely to be
	  7. Calling for the lost person		

	(c) 'Finding'—a sense of continual presence of deceased
	  —clear visual memory
	  —visual illusions		

	(d) Anger and guilt
	  —General irritability and bitterness
	  —Seeking to blame someone		

Late 'despair' phase	Depression
	  —Sadness
	  —Apathy
	  —Insomnia
	  —Anorexia
	  —Social withdrawal
		Develops in first month	Often maximal in second half of first year
			Usually resolves by two years

prescribed drugs in bereavement, if used at all, should be for a short duration only.

Bereavement care can be shared with other members of the practice team, and most hospices regularly include follow-up as part of their service. Some are developing schemes of training and using volunteer visitors. The grieving need practical help in the early stages where numbness and shock prevent the tackling of even the simplest tasks such as dealing with the death certificate or arranging the funeral. They will also need openness from their helpers to allow them to share their feelings and express their grief. They will need reassurance that the intensity and strangeness of their symptoms do not mean they are losing their sanity, and they will need support in surmounting the hurdles associated with resolution. National organizations such as Cruse for widows may have local groups providing support. The Society for Compassionate Friends is a self-help group for parents who have lost a child. For those 'tempted to suicide or despair', the Samaritans offer a 'befriending service'.

HOME CARE PROVISION

Taking into account the benefits of dying at home, there is room for discussion as to the most appropriate way of providing that care. This has been summarized by Ward (1982).

St. Christopher's Hospice in 1969 developed a domiciliary service sending specialist nurses into patient's homes to assist the primary care team. Unlike the development in the United States where similar services operating in the community have no inpatient facilities, in the UK most have attached inpatient units. These, as in the situation described by Prue Clench in Chapter 2, might be allowed to evolve, beginning with the funding by the National Society for Cancer Relief, of 'Macmillan nurses' working in the community, to the eventual provision of beds to back up the service. The survey by Lunt and Hillier (1981) showed that in 1980, 72 such services were operating (see Table 1.7). Furthermore, by May 1983, 93 services were listed by the British Hospice Information Centre (Clench 1984). This evolution of a community-based service to one providing inpatient facilities enables the primary care team to maintain their traditional clinical role, with referral to specialists where appropriate. Schemes originating in hospital wards and seeking to move into the community (Bates 1982) are less likely to be as acceptable to general practitioners. The type of service operating at St. Joseph's Hospice, Hackney, which undertakes the total care of the patient, although probably appropriate to inner city situations, would not be reproducible throughout the country.

One point seems undeniable, that successful home care requires the availability of beds to relieve the overstretched family and allow the dying patient to remain at home for as much time as possible.

Some general practitioners (25 per cent; Cartwright *et al*. 1973) have direct access to National Health Service (NHS) beds; of these, 85 per cent said they would like more. Seventy-one per cent of general practitioners questioned who had no such access, said they would like some. The reported use of a general practitioner hospital for terminal care in Peebles (Lyon and Love 1984) illustrates that general practitioners can maintain clinical responsibility for 68 per cent of their patients dying of cancer. The small number of home deaths in their sample (26 per cent compared with 40 per cent reported by Parkes 1978) might be explained by the ready access to hospital beds which general practitioners units provide. This explanation could be supported by the canvassed opinion of the general practitioners in Cartwright *et al*.'s study as to the facilities required, and as to the difficulty experienced in arranging admissions for patients with terminal illness (see Tables 1.8 and 1.9). In seeking to interpret the 1969 data obtained by interviewing, it should be borne in mind that oral morphine has only been gaining acceptance in the last decade, and the Macmillan nursing scheme only began to operate in 1978. Both these trends would make home care today more feasible for the patient and relatives. It ought to be noted, however, that admissions are often necessary for failure of night care, and, as mentioned in Chapter 4, an organized night-sitter service would be an important development. There would also seem to be further scope for expanding the availability of beds to general practitioners, at the same time as increasing the expertise in the community through Macmillan nurse teams.

Table 1.7. Specialist services in operation in December 1980

Administering body	Combination of services						Total
	IPU alone	IPU + HCT	IPU + HCT + HST	HCT alone	HCT + HST	HST	
NHS	14	6	1	5	4	1	31
Sue Ryder Foundation	5	1*	–	–	–	–	6
Marie Curie Foundation	10	–	–	–	–	–	10
Independent charity	8	10	1	3	1	–	23
Private nursing home	2	–	–	–	–	–	2
Total	39	17	2	8	5	1	72

IPU, inpatient unit; HCT, home care team; HST, hospital support team.
*This home care team is administratively within the NHS, though associated with a non-NHS inpatient unit.
From Lunt and Hillier (1981).

Table 1.8. General practitioner's views on facilities needed in their area

	Needed at all (%)	Needed most (%)
Short-term general hospital beds	47	8
Chronic hospital beds	86	29
Geriatric beds	89	51
Mental hospital places	34	2
District nurse services	24	2
Home help services	55	8
Number of general practitioners (=100%)	319	303

From Cartwright *et al.* (1973).

Table 1.9. Difficulty in arranging admission and number of domiciliary consultants

Estimated number of domiciliary consultations in last 12 months for patients with terminal illnes	Score of difficulty in arranging admission (%)					All general practitioners (%)
	0 or 1	2	2	4 or 5	6+	
None	52	43	25	26	27	32
1–4	35	41	59	47	44	46
5+	13	16	16	27	29	22
Number of general practitioners (=100%)	31	44	51	113	66	305

From Cartwright *et al. (1973).*

However, it is appropriate to raise the questions Tony Smith asks in his *British Medical Journal* leading article 'Problems of hospices' (1984):

Should the care of the dying be part of the NHS? or should it be part NHS, part private sector? If the private sector is to provide for much of the future expansion of terminal care, who will plan the siting of new units? Who will set standards of staffing and performance? If, on the other hand, the NHS is to take on the responsibility, will enough new money be found to provide both capital and revenue costs? Or will the sorry story of end stage renal failure be repeated, with never enough money to treat the patients in need? Secondly, whether in NHS or private units, whose responsibility should be the training of staff?

A crucial question to add is: What is the role of the general practitioner in the care of the dying at home, hospice, or hospital?

THE ROLE OF THE GENERAL PRACTITIONER

The role of the general practitioner in terminal care have been summarized elsewhere (Spilling 1982). The general practitioner's primary task lies in the consultation which, in terminal care, may need to be more directive. Cartwright *et al.* (1973) have shown that patients may not volunteer questions if they assess, perhaps incorrectly, that 'nothing could be done' or were embarrassed by their condition. The following examples were cited:

'Knew he couldn't do anything'. (loss of appetite and sarcoma of femur)
'It was part of his illness and nothing could be done for his conditions'. (depression in carcinoma of the prostate)
'We never discussed it. Mother was distressed'. (unpleasant smell)

Doctors were less likely to be consulted if they appear busy or uninterested. A summary of Cartwright *et al.*'s findings is shown in Fig. 1.1. It

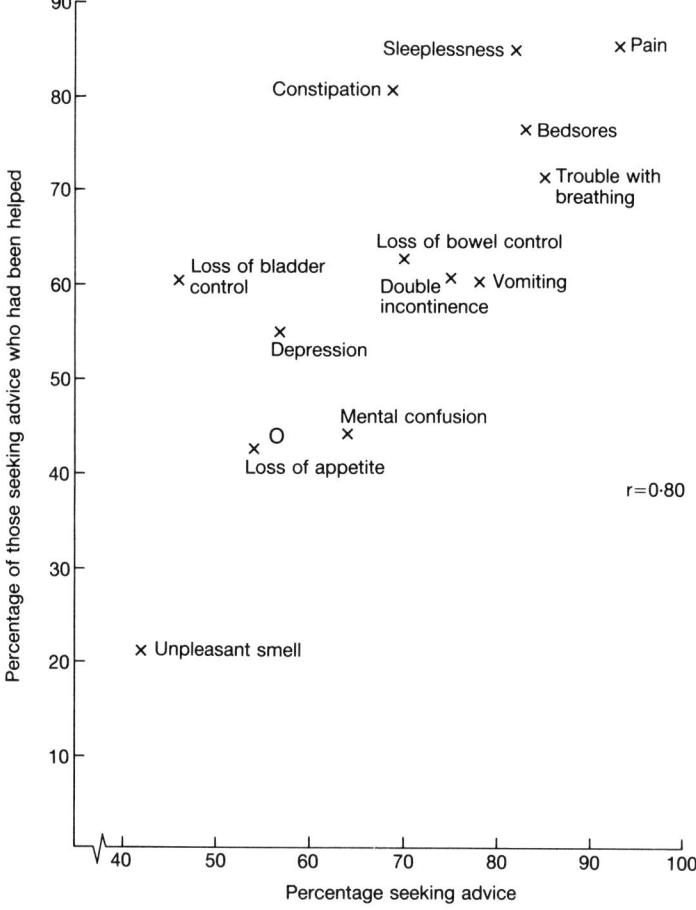

Fig. 1.1. Relationship between proportion consulting about different symptoms and proportion helped when they did consult. (From Cartwright *et al.* 1973.)

The role of the general practitioner 15

will be seen that pain is the problem most often presented and most often relieved. A useful aid to recording answers to direct questioning of the patient's pain is Robert Twycross's body chart shown in Fig. 2.

The general practitioner's additional role as co-ordinator of the various sources of help was further studied by Cartwright *et al.* (1973), and their conclusion is worth repeating here.

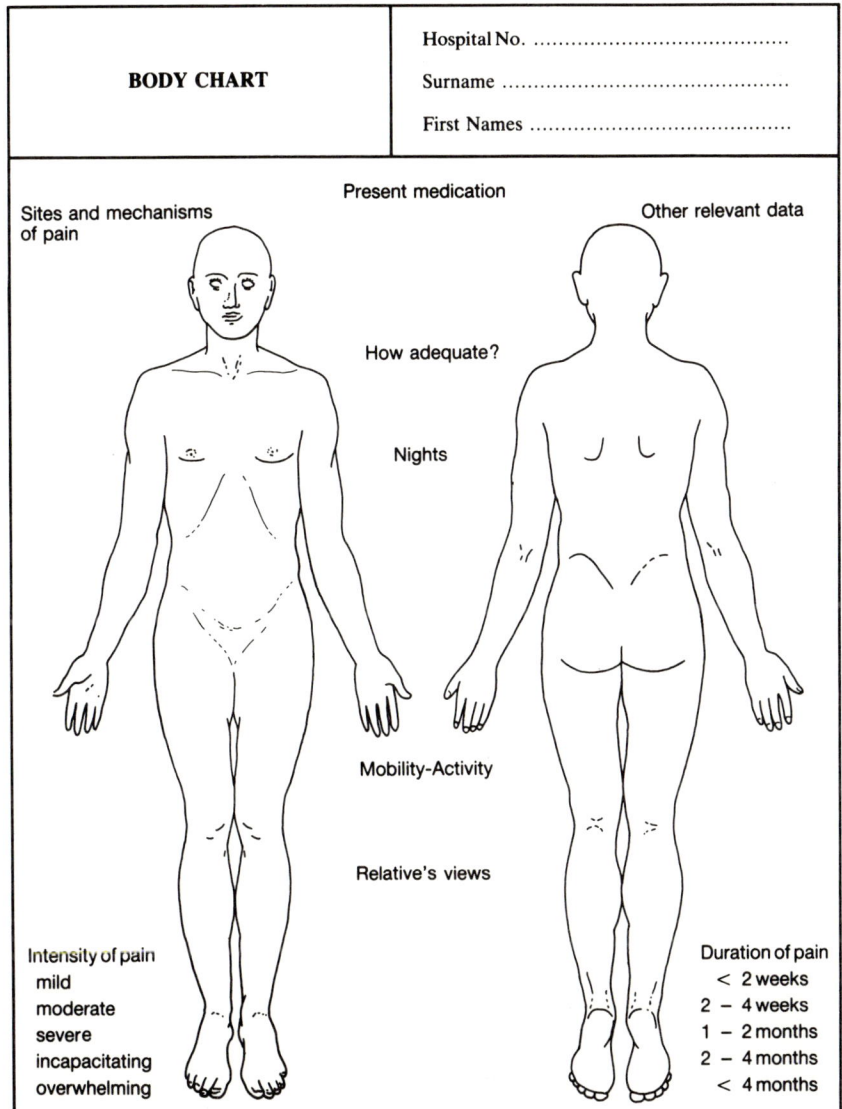

Fig. 1.2. Body chart. (From R. G. Twycross.)

The general practitioner plays a key role in the care of the dying. He gave nearly all the medical care to about three-tenths of the people in our sample in the last year of their lives and he usually looked after the other seven-tenths before they were admitted to hospital and arranged for their admission. He made many visits to those who had been in hospital, but came home to die . . . failure to recognise needs for community services which can help relatives and friends and the care of patients at home, suggest that general practitioners do not give as much support as they might to caring relatives, nor do the doctors seem to appreciate the amount of care that relatives and friends provide, or the extent and full nature of patients' needs in the last year of their lives.

THE GENERAL PRACTITIONER'S TRAINING

The important book published in 1972 by the Royal College of General Practitioners entitled *The future general practitioner*, included the objective for trainee general practitioners 'to discuss from experience the problems of home care and terminal cancer' (p. 67). Similar objectives were identified for the management of bereavement (pp. 131–3). Training schemes for general practitioners throughout the country have included study days in these two areas. Some vocational schemes include a rotation for a few months to a terminal care unit, most of which have domiciliary services attached. The future general practitioner should be well versed in appropriate care.

However, successful terminal care at home will also require the co-operation and understanding of hospital colleagues. They decide the timing and the patients for discharge from hospital beds. It is encouraging that the recommendation of the Wilkes report (1980*b*) to include terminal care in undergraduate medical training is being heeded. Reports from Belfast (Irwin 1984) illustrate the inter-disciplinary nature of the teaching, and similar courses are being piloted in other medical schools including that in Oxford. Future hospital doctors should be more informed than their predecessors, who it is hoped, will meet some of the findings of Cartwright *et al*'s survey (1973):

The knowledge and experience on which the decision to discharge terminally ill is made is even more questionable. Three-fifths of the general practitioners were critical about consultations over discharge. Lack of consultatations or assessment of home circumstances and delays in communication were sommon complaints.

CONCLUSION

Even though the control of pain in the home has been shown to be less effective than in hospital or hospice (Parkes 1985), only 3 per cent of relatives of patients who had died at home subsequently wished that the death had occurred in hospital (Wilkes 1984). Conversely, only 62 per cent of those who died in a hospice apparently 'wanted admission' while the rest had accepted only reluctantly (Parkes 1980).

The aim of this book is to enable all branches of the medical profession to meet more effectively the wishes of the population we serve. Cartwright *et al.* (1973) concludes:

Our health and social services may have partially mitigated the crude workings of the inverse care law; 'the availability of good ... care tends to vary inversely with the need of the population served' but the law could be reformulated; the availability of good care tends to vary inversely with the number of people suffering from a condition. And we all die.

Death belongs to life as birth does. The walk is in the raising of the foot as in the laying of it down

Rabindranath Tagore
Stray Birds

REFERENCES

Age Concern (1974). *Attitudes of retired and elderly*. Age Concern, London.

Aitken-Swan, J. (1959). Nursing the late cancer patient at home. *Practitioner* **183**, 64.

Ariès, P. (1976). *Western attitudes towards death from the Middle Ages to the present*. Marion Boyars, London.

Bates, T. (1982). 'At home and in the ward', *The dying patient*, (E. Wilkes ed.), MTP Press, London.

Bowlby, J. (1975). Attachment and loss In *Separation* Vol. 2, p. 110. Penguin Harmondsworth.

Byrne, S. R., Frances Dominica and Baum, J. D. (1984). Helen House—a hospice for children. Analysis of the first year. *British Medical Journal* **289**, 1665

Cartwright, A., Hockey, L. and Anderson, J. (1973). *Life before death*. Routledge and Kegan Paul, London.

Clench, P. (1984). *Managing to care in community services for the terminally ill*. Patten Press, Richmond.

Cotton, M., Cotton, G. and Goodall, J. (1981). A brother dies at home. *Maternal and Child Health* **6**, 288–92.

Durkheim, E. (1897). *Suicide*. (Translated by J. A. Spaulding and G. Simpson, 1952). Routledge, London.

Goffman, E. (1961). *Asylums*. Penguin, Harmondsworth.

Hawkes, J. (1952). *A guide to prehistoric and Roman antiquities of England and Wales*. Chatto and Windus, London.

Hughes, H. L. G. (1960). *Peace at the last*. Calouste Gulbenkian Foundation, London.

Illich, I. (1976). *Limits To Medicine*. Penguin, Harmondsworth.

Irwin, W. G. (1984). Teaching terminal care at Queen's University of Belfast. *British Medical Journal* **289**, 1509–11; 1604–5.

Kastenbaum, R. and Aisenberg, R. (1972). *The psychology of death*. Duckworth, London.

Lorenz, K. (1963). *On aggression*. Methuen, London.

Lunt, B. and Hillier, R. (1981). Terminal care; present services and future priorities. *British Medical Journal* **283**, 569.

Lyon, A. and Love, D. R. (1984). Terminal care—the role of the G. P. hospital. *Journal of the Royal College of General Practitioners* **263**, 331–3.

Munnichs, J. M. A. (1966). *Old age and finitude*. Karger, Basle and New York.

Parkes, C. M. (1978). Home or hospital. *Journal of the Royal College of General Practitioners* **28** 19–30.

—— (1980). Terminal care: evaluation of an advisory domiciliary service at St. Christopher's Hospice. *Postgraduate Medical Journal* **56** 685–9.

—— (1985). Terminal care—home, hospital or hospice? *Lancet***1**, 155–7.

Pritchard, P. (1975). Community participation in primary health care. *Brith Medical Journal* **2**, 583.

RCGP (1981). Patient participation in primary health care. Occasional paper, **17** Royal College of General Practitioners, London.

Robertson, J. (1953). Some responses of young children to loss of maternal care. *Nursing Times***49**, 382.

Rossman, I. and Kissick, W. L. (1961). Home care and the cancer patient. From *The physician and the total care of the cancer patient*. American Cancer Society, New York.

Sagov, S. S. (1984). *Home Birth*. Aspen. Costello, Tunbridge Wells.

Saunders, C. (1959). *Care of the dying*. Macmillan, London. *British Medical Journal* **288**, 1178.

Smith, T. (1984). Problems of hospices. *British Medical Journal* **288**, 1178.

Spilling, R. (1982). In *Geriatric problems in general practice* (G. Wilcock, J. Gray and P. Pritchard, eds). Oxford University Press.

Stoddart, S. (1979). *The Hospice Movement*. Jonathan Cape, London.

Toynbee, A. (1968). *Man's concern with death*. Hodder and Stoughton, London.

Ward, A. (1982). Standards for home care services for the terminally ill. *Community Medicine*, **4**, 276.

Wilkes, E. (1980a). *Hospice in Britain*. International conference, St. Christopher's Hospice, June 1980.

—— (1980b). *Standing medical advisory committee. Report of a working group on terminal care*. Department of Health and Social Security, London.

—— (1984). Dying now. **Lancet 1**, 950–2.

2 The development of home care services in the UK

Prue Clench

THE DEMAND

Since the early 1970s the demand for hospice care has steadily increased to epidemic proportions. The funding of the majority of services relies heavily on public support and it is necessary to examine the underlying reasons for their popularity.

Several factors are relevant: the somewhat impersonal care received by patients arising from the modern preoccupation in hospital medicine with the disease rather than the individual, and overstretched community services and reduced staff hours which contribute to fragmented management and poor liaison. The public have been made aware through the media that much of the physical distress and anxiety associated with terminal illness, especially cancer, can be lessened by the approach demonstrated by hospices, and communities all over the country are determined to provide such an amenity in their area. At the heart of this commitment are those who have lacked the support they needed whilst nursing a dying relative or have experienced at first hand the benefits of hospice care.

Whilst the public tend to associate hospice care with a building, the appointment of some 300 Macmillan nurses to visit patients in general hospitals and in their own homes has brought the knowledge and skills of the hospice into the general management of many patients' care. The generous backing of the National Society for Cancer Relief (NSCR) in funding Macmillan nurses, in association with about 70 health authorities, has enabled general practitioners and district nurses to prove the value to them of the additional support given to the family. Also, the practical help and advice on modern methods of symptom control enables many more of their patients to spend their last days at home.

Since 1982 I have been involved in over 250 discussions with general practitioners, community nurses, and health authority officials in different parts of the UK. These discussions have reinforced my conviction that the role of the clinical nurse specialist in terminal care, working within the primary care team, is the most appropriate one in the long term. This situation results in cultivating better support for all terminally ill patients through shared care, hand-in-hand with training programmes. The obvious financial advantages of establishing home care teams to complement existing services, as opposed to the prohibitive cost of inpatient care, have made this development widely welcomed within the National Health Services (NHS). However, the essential role of strategic hospice units with fully-developed facilities for teaching, research, and ongoing training of specialist staff on a national scale should not be overlooked.

TYPES AND TRENDS IN COMMUNITY SERVICES

The mainstays of homecare teams, whether based at a hospital, hospice, or in the community, are nurses who are often the only full-time members. Their role relates specifically to the needs of patients and families facing death and bereavement, working closely with other health professionals and striving to raise the standard of terminal care within the area served. The way in which such teams operate will depend upon the model chosen and local factors.

Home care services

The opening of St. Christopher's Hospice, London in 1967 was followed two years later by the introduction of a team to visit patients in their own homes and extend the help available to general practitioners and district nurses, both within and outside the Hospice. Until the mid-1970s it was felt that hospice beds were an essential component of this care, thus restricting development of home care services to those based at special units.

Hospital support teams

In 1977 St. Thomas' Hospital, London introduced the concept of the hospital support team, offering shared care on the wards and extending this into the community.

Domiciliary care services

Whilst the need for access to hospital beds has always been recognized, the financial difficulties in meeting the running costs in the face of the 1974 cuts in NHS expenditure caused a number of projects to adopt a phased approach. First, to introduce a home care team (usually referred to as a domiciliary care service), followed by day care, and ultimately an inpatient unit according to proven need and viability. The first of these projects was the Dorothy House Foundation, which serves the Bath Health District. An account of its development follows, as it illustrates what can be achieved with modest resources and gives substance to the claims propounded in this chapter.

These nurses, often referred to as Macmillan nurses, have been funded by the NSCR for the first three years. The Society does not exercise a direct management responsibility but has established basic criteria in selecting staff, who must hold a community qualification and attend the English National Board Course 931 on 'The continuing care of the dying patient and the family'. Marie Curie nurses are recruited with the co-operation of each district health authority and utilized on an agency basis, funded jointly by the health authority and the Marie Curie Memorial Foundation. Appropriate orientation and support is being introduced in many areas.

THE DEVELOPMENT OF THE DOROTHY HOUSE FOUNDATION

The Dorothy House Foundation (later a Macmillan service) was founded in May 1976 to augment the care available to patients in the terminal phase of illness and to support the whole family during this time and in bereavement. It seeks to create awareness of the needs of dying patients and provide opportunities for developing skills for professional staff and members of the community. It works in close co-operation with the Bath District Health Authority to supplement the existing services and facilities

Table 2.1. Types and distribution of services in the community

In May 1983 there were 93 services listed by the British Hospice Information Centre as offering support to terminally ill patients in hospital and/or their own homes. These can be broadly categorized as follows:

Type		No.	%
Home care service (HCS)	Based at a hospice/unit	25	27
Domiciliary care service (DCS/C)	Based in the community	40	43
Domiciliary care service (DCS/H)	Based at a hospital	7	7
Domiciliary care service (DCS/U)	Based at a special unit but relating to the primary care team	9	10
Hospitals (HST/H)	Based within the hospital	8	9
Hospital support team (HST/C)	as above but also involved in the community	4	4

Within 12 months of completing this survey the number of services had risen by 23% of which 59% of these related to the appointment of clinical nurse specialists to work in the community and/or hospital.

22 The development of home care services

available in the District. Initially, no NHS funds were available and the Foundation registered as a charity being encouraged by the enthusiasm and support of local people. The work is founded upon trust in God's guidance and provision, as denoted in its name 'Dorothy' meaning 'gift of God', and is managed by a council. Its income is derived from many sources, mainly generated by the local community with welcome assistance from several trusts, Bath District Health Authority, and the NSCR.

The domiciliary service was inaugurated in January 1977 with one nurse and then a secretary, and help was given to 81 families in the first year. The service has been steadily extended in response to demand and is now used by the majority of general practitioners in the Bath Health District. The District includes parts of Avon, Somerset, and Wiltshire, with a population of around 365 000, of whome 81 000 live in the city of Bath. Using 1975 figures supplied by the Wessex Regional Cancer Organisation as a baseline, the Foundation has increased its involvement in the care of terminally ill cancer patients within the District from 7 per cent in the first year to 33 per cent in 1984. Medical and nursing management of patients' care has always remained with the primary care team, to which the domiciliary nurse attaches herself by mutual consent.

Day care was initiated during the first year on a purely social basis. Patients, with or without their relatives, were invited to coffee or tea at the house that served as a base. The same house was also used for 'Evenings for bereaved families', which were held bi-monthly and attended by about 80 people. Since the conversion of these premises into a small inpatient unit, day care has been expanded to cater for seven patients on two days a week. The programme is organized by a part-time physiotherapist, assisted by a rota of volunteer helpers and drivers who bring patients from a wide area. This has proved to be a most valuable and cost-effective way of giving extra support to needy families.

The Assessment Unit with six beds was opened in October 1979. As the District is well-provided with community hospitals, only a small number of beds were required, primarily to offer specialist assistance in managing difficult symptoms and stabilizing patients' care on a short-stay basis, although those patients who need to remain until their death are able to do so. Many patients who die in the Unit have been able to return home prior to their final admission. Due to the prior establishment of the domiciliary service, only very few patients have been referred to admission a few days before their death and the Unit's function has not been abused or misunderstood, as has been the experience of many new hospices.

Volunteers have shared in every aspect of the service from its inception and continue to make a valuable contribution in all departments. They are co-ordinated by a volunteers' organizer, and much care is taken in their

Table 2.2. Evaluation of the service

Questionaires were sent to 77 doctors (including 59 practices), 80 nurses and 13 social workers: 81 percent returned completed forms. (figures are shown in percentages.)

Should the service be:	Discontinued	Maintained	Expanded	No comment
Doctors	3	19	71	7
Community nurses	–	–	77	23
Hospital nurses	–	14	81	5
Social workers	–	–	92	8

Value of the unit:	Undesirable	Essential	Desirable	Optional
Doctors	3	30	44	13
Community nurses	–	41	40	19
Hospital nurses	–	43	48	9
Social workers	–	58	33	9

A strong contingent of the surveyed group believed that the services of the Dorothy House Foundation have an educational role. This belief was underwritten by 100 percent of community nurses and social workers, for whom an educational role is primary. Hospital nurses (95 percent) endorsed this and 68 percent of doctors regoznized this aspect of the work.

Patients (15) were asked to rate what aspect of the service they had found most helpful. Questionnaires were returned anonymously.

Friendship and moral support	14
Drugs/treatment advice	11
Explanation of illness	11
Support of their relatives	11
Telephone support after hours	10
Practical assistance	9
Financial advice	4
Social excursions	3

selection, preparation, and support. Equal emphasis is placed upon the need for volunteers in the care of families, administrative duties, and fund-raising.

The education programme, as an essential component of this type of service, has striven to accommodate the many and varied demands for talks, visits, information, placements, seminars, and courses. This has been greatly facilitated, since 1980, by the addition of Macmillan House, which is adjacent to the Assessment Unit, and the appointment of a full-time clinical teacher. The Foundation has served as a centre for the 'Care of the dying patient and his family' course for nurses and arranges visits for general practitioner trainees, social workers, and clergy.

Table 2.3. Statistical review of the Dorothy House Foundation

Patients:	1977	1979	1981	1983	1984	Domiciliary:	1977	1981	1983	1984
Current 1 Jan.		37	87	103	121	Team members	1	5.1	5.6	6.5
New referrals	81	203	242	336	300	Case-load per team	20	85	113	130
Total visited	81	240	329	439	421	Case-load of full time member/p.a.	81	65	78	64
Referred by: (%)						Length of referral (%)				
GP	34	34	50	54	58	Under a week		4	10	
Community nurse	25	23	11	12	13	1–3 weeks		40	28	
Hospital staff		7	9	8	10	4–10 weeks		37	31	
Social worker	29	23	20	21	15	11–26 weeks		15	16	
Other	12	13	10	5	4	Over one year		–	7	
Age (%)						Status (%)				
Under 30 years	5	1	2	1	2	Male	30	46	48	49
30–45	9	7	6	7	7	Married	60	73	63	63
46–70	53	47	52	58	64	Div./single	14	10	10	9
Over 70 years	33	45	40	34	27	Widowed	26	17	27	28

The development of the Dorothy House Foundation

Outcome (%)					
Current 1 Dec.	11	24	23	28	24
Discharged	12	7	4	5	10
Died	77	69	73	67	66
Place of death (%)					
Hospital	50		39	39	40
Hospice		50	18	18	19
Home			43	43	41
Hospice (%)					
Actual admissions		23[1]	104	105	125
Dom. referrals		65	91	99	94
Direct admission		13	5	—	—
Hospital transfer		22	4	1	6
Total case-load		9	27	22	30
Outcome (%)					
Discharged home			52	42	51
Transferred			4	7	6
Died			44	51	43
Average stay (days)			15	13	12
Average bed occupancy			74	67	70
Day care:					
No. of sessions			201	259	525 (restricted by premises)
Visits: Mileage					
Av. visits per patient			14	12	13
Av. miles per visit			10	9	8
Mileage per nurse p.a. (Bath)					8000
Mileage per nurse p.a. (rural)					15 000

[1] Hospice opened 1 October 1979.

The administration is handled by a small, dedicated team, which provides the vital back-up to this expanding organization and is the central hub that co-ordinates all activities. The staff are in touch with the public, without whose support the scope of the service would diminish.

The advisory committee consists of senior officers in the Health Service who advise the Foundation on matters affecting the care of patients in relation to other services in the District. A high degree of collaboration exists between the Health Authority and Dorothy House, and the domiciliary nurses were incorporated into the Community Nursing Division in April 1983, although their management remains the responsibility of the Foundation. In due course it is hoped that the Authority may be able to increase the funding of their salaries. Table 2.3 indicates the overall contribution that has been made.

HOW DO THESE TEAMS FUNCTION IN RELATION TO THE PRIMARY CARE TEAM?

The nurse's role is to work alongside members of the primary care team in whatever way may be appropriate. This may consist of providing time for the patient or relative to talk, mobilizing practical help and involving volunteers, participating in the monitoring of symptoms and suggesting medication that may be more effective, sharing in planning the patient's care on a 24-hour, seven day a week basis, and offering practical nursing care or administering drugs if necessary. She has an important role in liaising closely with all involved in the patient's care and acts as a catalyst in applying the principles of care developed in the hospices to patients in their own homes.

The hospice-based home care service

This usually comprises of a doctor who has specialized in terminal care and who is involved in the care of patients both in the hospice and in the community, two or more nurses who work specifically with patients able to be looked after at home, and, depending on the resources of the organization, other professionals such as a chaplain, social worker, etc. Referrals are usually accepted only from the general practitioner by the hospice doctor and will specify what kind of help and advice is requested. Individual members of the team may be involved exclusively in particular circumstances, but the advantages of a multidisciplinary consultation are well recognized.

With regard to prescribing and reviewing medication, this is usually supervised by the hospice doctor in close liaison with the general practitioner. The patient's condition is monitored by the home care nurses, who also keep in touch with the district nurse and doctors.

Advantages

The advice of a doctor who has specialized in terminal care will obviously assist the general practitioner in managing symptoms of a more difficult nature.

Such teams, as part of the hospice staff, can readily arrange admission for patients when necessary, allowing maximum flexibility of care provision.

Nurses in these teams usually prefer shared case-loads and receive better peer support and leadership.

Many teams operate a 24-hour on-call service in which staff participate on a rota basis. This is particularly advantageous in deprived inner city areas where such calls may include routine nursing duties.

Disadvantages

The referral policy can be over-reliant on the general practitioner's awareness of the needs of the patient and/or his family, especially when a service is new and all that can be achieved is not appreciated. Many doctors fear that the involvement of the hospice will confuse families or cause the patient to give up hope. Some general practitioners are reluctant to involve the hospice doctor unless they are encountering problems in controlling a patient's symptoms or require an admission. This results in late referrals and can lead to the team being predominantly associated with pre-admission and post-discharge patients.

The role of the home care team sometimes arouses resentment amongst colleagues if it is felt that it erodes the relationship of the patient with their own doctor and district nurse.

Whilst great importance is attached to liaison with members of the primary care team, management is often felt to have been transferred to the specialists, particularly if they operate an on-call system.

The hospital support teams

These are usually available to the primary care team as well as ward staff. They operate on the basis of shared care, aiming to complement existing services and educate on the job. Referrals are made by the general practitioner or hospital consultant. The doctor or houseman write-up all medication and their role is in no way diminished.

The team usually consists of one or two full-time nurses, with part-time availability of a doctor with specialist experience in terminal care, a social worker, chaplain, and secretary, although this may not be achieved initially.

Advantages and disadvantages

Once again, the small financial outlay involved can improve the care within the setting of the general hospital where, at present, more than 65 per cent of patients die.

The teams teach on the wards, where medical students and student nurses are most influenced.

Liaison between hospital and community staff is a major factor in the success or failure of these teams, and extreme care must be taken in bridging the traditional demarcation line. In inner-city areas where it is less practical to contact personally all concerned in a patient's care, more time should be spent initially introducing team members to community staff.

The community-based domiciliary service

The domiciliary service usually begins with the appointment of two nurses with District Nurse or Health Visitor qualifications, who are seconded to attend the six-week English National Board Course 931, which provides a basic foundation to what must be an ongoing training programme.

The nurses usually have contracts with the district health authority, even if funded from charitable sources, and are members of the Community Nursing Division, based at NHS premises where they are readily accessible to their colleagues and take part in meetings arranged for all staff. Two main features distinguish them from other district nurses: due to the specific nature of their appointment, they can offer unhurried support to patients and relatives, at the discretion of the family doctor and community nurse. As specialists, they have a responsibility to be up-to-date with new developments. They form a resource within the district with an important educational role.

Referals are usually welcomed from any professional involved in the patient's care but will not be accpeted without the consent of the patient's own doctor. This should be sought by visiting the general practitioner and discussing what help might be required and whether the involvement of the domiciliary nurse is desired. On the basis of the discussion with both the doctor and group-attached district nurse, it will become more apparent how the domiciliary nurse can contribute without duplication. Close liaison will foster good relationships and team-work and enhance the support received by patient and family. It takes time for a new team to be accepted and much will depend upon the members' tact and personality. However, once the value of their contribution has been recognized, the demand far exceeds their resources—a matter warranting comment later in this chapter.

Medication is prescribed by the general practitioner. As the knowledge of the principles of effective symptom control acquired by the domiciliary nurse is appreciated, she will be invited to make suggestions regarding medication. Awareness of the problems grows from accurate monitoring and reporting by the nurses, and encouraging results are often achieved by closer supervision of the drugs prescribed. Both doctors and nurses gain confidence through small successes and develop their own skills through involvement with colleagues experienced in this field.

The patient's care remains the responsibility of the primary care team at all times, and the domiciliary nurse supplements their services as appropriate. This may include practical nursing care on an ad hoc basis or by mutual agreement with the district nurse.

Advantages

There is little doubt that this model is the most acceptable to doctors and nurses in the community and is favoured by the NHS management. It enhances the care given to a larger number of patients without eroding the traditional roles of other carers and produces encouraging results from quite a small financial outlay.

It provides a good base from which to expand the team and makes maximum use of existing services and personnel. Its potential is now widely recognized and therefore more likely to be allocated funds, either by a health authority or charity.

Disadvantages

It takes time to convince colleagues about how the patient's care can be improved, especially in the area of medication. Ignorance, prejudice, and old wives' tales abound and patients are commonly prescribed inappropriate or inadequate analgesics, narcotics by injection when they can swallow without difficulty, and the antiquated Brompton Mixture. Nevertheless, the situation does improve in due course and interest and commitment grow.

Domiciliary nurses usually carry their own case-loads and do not routinely introduce other team nurses or provide an on-call service in the formal sense of the term. They offer their home telephone number to families, who derive much comfort from the knowledge that they may ring if they are in difficulties, and this arrangement is seldom if ever abused. Emergency calls usually relate to physical crises, which continue to be dealt with by the general practitioner. However, the adequacy of this support depends upon the availability of local services and level of co-operation with other members of the primary care team. This also applies to other times when the domiciliary nurse may not be available, such as during holiday or study leave, when another member of the team may not be desired by the patient or family unless problems occur. It is the responsibility of the nurse to make sure that colleagues are aware of her absence and date of return and that the patient and carer know to whom to turn if the need arises.

Within the first year success may result in the number of referrals exceeding the resources of the pilot scheme. The domiciliary nurses are notoriously bad at saying 'No' and colleagues can be dismissive about the service if their request can not be met immediately. It is essential that the nurse manager mediates in this situation and directs the demand for more nurses through the appropriate channels.

The domiciliary nurses may feel very isolated, especially if they were not previosuly working as community nurses in the same area. They need peer support, as well as enlightened management, and may have to travel quite long distances to meet colleagues facing the same problems.

WHAT DO TEAMS OFFER THE GENERAL PRACTITIONER?

Access to a home care team places at the general practitioner's disposal various resources in the care of his terminally ill patients, which can be summarized as follows:

1. Trained staff with additional knowledge and experience, who are able to spend more time with the family and report on any change in the home situation, mobilizing support of all kinds and assisting members of the primary care team as required.
2. A greater degree of informal and individualized care than can normally be arranged.
3. A service that bridges gaps to ensure continuity of care, including bereavement follow-up.
4. The kind of flexible help, making maximum use of public and voluntary resources, that builds up the confidence of patient and relative, enabling them to manage at home without the stress and exhaustion otherwise encountered.

It may also include access to day care and hospice beds for those with special needs. As skills and co-operation grow, it facilitates the type of care associated with hospices and specialist units to be achieved in the patient's own home, without diminishing the relationship between the patient and those who have cared for him throughout his illness.

Time

Most people are very aware of the number of patients the doctor has to see and the fact that, however caring and conscientious, he cannot spare the sort of time on a regular basis that it takes to share the whole spectrum of thoughts and reactions through which patients and their families may pass when faced with terminal illness. Consequently, they tend to mention only physical symptoms, for which the doctor can prescribe some medication, and leave unsaid the fears, questions, hopes, and heartaches, that constitute the true measure of distress.

It takes time to build-up the kind of communication that allows everything to be shared at random and the professional must be a good listener, skilled at creating a relaxed and unhurried approach and demonstrating genuine concern without intrusion. Obviously, a doctor who has known the family over many years will find it easier to build on this foundation. For many today, this is no longer the norm.

It takes time to assess the patients' overall condition and the extent to which they are coping at home. This is best observed whilst carrying out the routine tasks of daily living, such as making tea or answering the doorbell, and by sensing the atmosphere in the household. Questions alone are seldom answered frankly, and time to observe unobtrusively in the context of a more social visit to the patient's own home will provide a truer picture. Several examples illustrate this point:

The woman who developed a very painful leg, who always remained seated during her doctor's visits and declared that she did not have any pain, the reason being that she lived alone and did not want him to think she could not manage and admit her to hospital; the man with severe pain for whom a narcotic analgesic was prescribed without any accompanying aperient, who subsequently denied having any pain rather than endure the miseries of constipation; the frail, elderly lady who 'forgot' to take 'the mixture' prescribed by the consultant, having seen a fellow patient in hospital commence a similar-looking concoction a few days before her death, rapidly deteriorate, and be moved to the side ward, 'never to be mentioned again'; lastly, the brave husband whose handicapped wife relied upon him, who denied all symptoms in a vain attempt to conceal the evidence that he could no longer manage her care.

Such are the ingredients of patients' real fears and without time to listen and observe we shall not hear about them until it is too late to relieve them.

Informal and individualized care

The general practitioner will rightly be associated with diagnosis, treatment and cure, and both he and his patient have to adjust to a new partnership to achieve the best quality of life remaining to that patient on his terms. The patient will need encouragement to share his wishes, which should no longer take second place to the dictates of treatment unless mutually considered worthwhile. Control over his circumstances and the management of his illness can be shared with him and will restore his self-respect and confidence. This process can be greatly assisted by the domiciliary nurse, who can communicate the patient's wishes to the appropriate members of the team and enable families to avail themselves of the range of services relevant to their needs, thus minimizing their feelings of helplessness.

During visits to the home, problems of a social nature become apparent. Who will meet the children from school? Fetch the prescription? Arrange for the dog to go into kennels whilst the patient who lives alone goes into hospital for treatment? How will the cost be met? How does the relative feel about nursing a very ill husband/mother? Are they on the telephone? Whilst most general practitioners are well aware of these domestic issues, neither they nor the district nurse always have time to mobilize the diversity of help that may be needed. It is the author's impression that as much avoidable distress is due to overlooking this aspect as is caused by poor management of physical symptoms, and it is largely attributable to the lack of time to give sufficient personal attention to each family in this situation.

Confidence to cope

It is surely fear on the part of the family, far more than physical strain, that contributes to a great number of patients being admitted to hospital during the last few days of their lives. The national average of patients with malignant disease who die in hospital is over 65 per cent. Anxiety rises to the level of near panic against a background of heavy nursing demands, maybe over many months, and the doctor suggests that the carer has 'done all you can' and the patient is admitted. This is in marked contrast with the proportion of patients who die at home, usually over 50 per cent of those referred, where the general practitioner has been able to involve a domiciliary care service.

Admission seldom achieves the relief intended. The patient is usually distressed to be removed from familiar surroundings. He does not want to be a burden to his relatives, but he may fear admission to a strange ward. Leaving home may mean parting with a pet that has been a source of great comfort, and facing the possibility that he may be leaving home for the last time. Relatives may not declare until after the death that they had promised the patient that he should remain at home; most patients and families view home as the best environment and feel regret if the death occurred in an institution, however pressing at the time the reasons for admission. The physical exhaustion of the carer will pass in due course, but regrets may remain and complicate bereavement.

Here surely is the crux of the problem. Relatives, even neighbours, manage to cope remarkably well, even caring for the patient over death itself, if they have confidence that help is at hand if needed. That confidence is built-up gradually before death is imminent and stems from the assurance given to the carer by the key member of the primary team that they may call upon them as they would a close friend, maybe at night or over a public holiday when other services are covered by reduced staff who may not be familiar with the patient. It matters little who the key person is, but it must be someone they know well and have come to trust. In recent years such commitment on the part of individuals has diminished, and there has been inevitable fragmentation of care through the introduction of evening and night nursing shifts, deputizing services for doctors, and the increase in health centres where patients may be expected to relate to several doctors. Home care and domiciliary services offer one way of overcoming these difficulties.

ESTABLISHING HOME CARE TEAMS

General practitioners and community nurses must be involved from the beginning in planning what is needed in their district and proposals should reflect the resources and skills available locally.

Education will be required about the role of the home care/domiciliary nurse in relation to traditional carers, and ample time must be allowed for discussion before the service is introduced.

Publicity will need to emphasize the complementary role of the proposed team, which does not supplant the family doctor or district nurse, and that the recourse to charitable funds does not indicate a lack of support from the health authority.

A management structure will be required and an operational policy agreed that looks beyond the appointment of two nurses, to the development of the service according to demand and resources. There must be professional commitment to the long-term future of the project to maintain its interests in the competitive world of local authority budgets.

Due care must be taken in setting-up guidelines about liaison, method of referral, availability of the nurses, catchment area, case-loads, and the expected date when the nurses' will be in post. It should be noted that following the appointment of the nurses they will be away on courses, and time should also be allowed on their return for them to introduce themselves and describe their new role to those with whom they will be working. It usually takes six to nine months before a new domiciliary nurse can accept a full case-load, i.e. 15–20 patients. From this it will be obvious that whilst the service will be intended to cover the whole district in due course, it cannot be widely available from the start. The reasons for initially appointing two nurses relate to available funding and the importance of protecting one nurse from the onerous responsibility of establishing a new service single-handed.

Regular review and factual reports will encourage recognition of the service and rectify unhelpful procedures. Communication should be encouraged between all concerned so that the project develops according to local need and remains flexible.

In conclusion, in no other area of patient care is the challenge so urgent for general practitioners to become involved in the establishment of these teams and to avail themselves of the help offered, or for the National Health Service to co-operate with charitable bodies to make provision nationally.

ACKNOWLEDGEMENTS

Some of this material has been previously published in my article Dying at Home, *Journal of District Nursing* pp. 21–4, July (1984), and in a handbook entitled *Managing to care in community services for the terminally ill* (1984), published by Patten Press, Richmond.

3 Symptom control

Robert Twycross

> To cure sometimes
> Relieve often
> Comfort always.

Comfort care, or symptom control, is an important and integral part of care of the dying. In the interests of brevity, the remarks in this chapter have been restricted to terminal cancer. The general principles are, however, more broadly applicable.

Patients with advanced cancer experience a wide variety of symptoms, though none is a constant feature (Table 3.1). Although a symptom is present, it need not be caused by the malignant disease *per se*. Causative factors include:

1. the cancer itself;
2. anti-cancer treatment;
3. non-specific association with debility;
4. concurrent second disorder.

Even when a symptom is caused by the cancer itself, different mechanisms may be operative and treatment for the same symptom may vary considerably from patient to patient. As many symptoms are caused by multiple factors, it is necessary to identify the different factors involved, and then to seek to correct those that are reversible. In this way, although

Table 3.1. Common symptoms on admission[1]

Pain	69
Anorexia	66
Constipation	46
Dry mouth	41
Nausea	38
Insomnia	37
Dyspnoea	34
Vomiting	32
Oedema	32
Cough	26

[1]Sir Michael Sobell House, Oxford, 1981. $n = 391$.

the underlying pathological process remains unchanged, it is usually possible to obtain significant, if not complete, relief.

Treatment begins with an explanation by the doctor of the reason(s) for each symptom. To learn that the doctor understands what is happening is reassuring and does much to reduce the impact of the symptom on the sufferer. If explanation is omitted, the patient continues to think that his condition is totally shrouded in mystery, and this is frightening. Often, it is appropriate to discuss treatment options with the patient and to decide together on the immediate course of action. Parallel explanation and discussion with the relatives is also important.

GENERAL CONSIDERATIONS

Treatment should not be limited to drugs

For example, an emollient cream (aqueous cream B.P., Boots E45) or a bland hand cream (Nivea) applied to dry, pruritic skin two or three times a day and the use of emulsifying ointment instead of soap will relieve pruritus in most patients. The use of an antihistamine (or of cholestyramine in obstructive jaundice) is of little value unless measures are taken to correct skin dryness.

Choice of drug

The choice of drug to relieve a given symptom is governed by a number of considerations. For example, the choice of an antiemetic depends on:

1. the underlying pathological mechanism;
2. whether used purely prophylactically, (e.g. when a narcotic is prescribed for the first time);
3. the severity of vomiting;
4. the degree of coexistent anxiety;
5. whether patient is drowsy;
6. the desirability of anticholinergic side-effects, (e.g. the drying up of saliva in patients with troublesome sialorrhoea).

When used to control a persistent symptom, a drug should be administered regularly and prophylactically (*not* 'as required'), and the dose titrated against effect.

Timing

Morphine sulphate needs to be given every four hours; most other drugs can be given less frequently. Although the duration of the effect of the drug is positively correlated with its plasma half-life, the relationship is not linear.

For example, when taken regularly, methadone has a half-life of between 20 and 60 hours, compared with 2–2.5 hours for morphine. Yet, the duration of the analgesic effect of methadone is generally only some 6–8 hours, that is, 1.5–2 times that of morphine. Even so, drugs with a longer plasma half-life generally need to be given less frequently, commonly only once or twice a day.

Supervision

With narcotic analgesics, psychotropic drugs, and laxatives in particular, it is not usually possible to predict exactly the optimum dose. Dose adjustments will therefore be necessary, especially during the first week or two. This should be anticipated and arrangements made for continuing close supervision. Whenever the prescription of an additional drug is considered, it is important to ask:

1. Is it possible for the patient to stop one or more of the preparations he is already taking?
2. Is it possible to substitute one drug for any two of those presently or about to be prescribed?

Precise guidelines are necessary to achieve maximum patient co-operation, particularly when narcotic analgesics are prescribed. 'Take as much as you like, as often as you like' is a recipe for anxiety, poor symptom control, and maximum side-effects. When morphine is prescribed, the need for a regular administration every four hours must be emphasized. The first and last dose of the day should be 'anchored' to the patient's waking and bedtime. The best additional times during the day are generally 10.00, 14.00, and 18.00 hours, unless the patient wakes or goes to bed exceptionally late (Figure. 3.1). The drug regimen should be written out in full for the patient and his family to work from, stating times to be taken, names of drugs, reason for use, ('for pain', 'for bowels', etc) and dose ($x$ml, y tablets). The patient and the family should be warned about possible initial side-effects and arrangements for follow-up confirmed.

Expectations

Although most symptoms respond completely or to a large extent to a combination of drug and non-drug measures, it is sometimes necessary to compromise in order to avoid unacceptable and unwanted effects; e.g. with tricyclics in depression, anticholinergic effects such as dry mouth or visual disturbance are occasionally limiting factors. In relation to bowel obstruction, it is often better to aim to reduce the incidence of vomiting to once or twice a day rather than to seek absolute control.

Tablets/medicines	2 am	On waking	10 am	2 pm	6 pm	Bedtime	28 March 1980 Purpose
Morphine (20 mg in 10 ml)	10	10	10	10	10	10	For pain
Flurbiprofen (tab. 50 mg)		1		1		1	For pain
Prednisolone (tab. 5 mg)			1	1	1		For appetite (Dissolve in water)
Dioctyl forte (tab. 100 mg)			1				For bowels
Dorbanex (capsules)			2				For bowels
Chlorpromazine (tab. 25 mg)						3	For sleep
Nystatin (liquid)		2	2	2	2	2	For mouth

Fig. 3.1. Medication list for patient's use at home. A more simple one is used by patients taking medication less frequently.

Increasing weakness, although it may be associated with severe anaemia, hypercalcaemia or paraplegia, often means that the battle against the malignant process has been lost. It is at this stage that the patient is forced to face the fact that death is inevitable. Equally, it is a time when support and companionship are of major importance. Although the doctor may feel powerless in the face of death, his continued attendance, indicating that he will stand by the patient no matter what happens, is of great value to the patient and the family, and to other staff.

PAIN CONTROL

About two-thirds of dying cancer patients experience pain the weeks or months prior to death. Possibly, a third of those cared for at home die still in pain. There are many reasons for inadequate relief. It is common for doctors to lose their systematic approach and objectivity when confronted with a dying patient. Instead of carefully analysing the cause(s) of the patient's pain(s), they dispense a standard prescription of some favourite preparation; or worse, they under-rate the intensity of a patient's discomfort and do nothing.

Diagnostic probabilities

A prospective survey of 100 cancer patients with pain admitted consecutively to Sir Michael Sobell House, Oxford, illustrates the pattern of pain in advanced cancer (Twycross and Fairfield 1982). The number of anatomically distinct pains in individual patients ranged from one to eight (Fig. 3.2). Eighty had more than one pain; 34 four or more. The total number of pains experienced was 303. In only 41 patients was all the pain caused by the cancer itself. In nine, no pain came into this category.

Of the pains caused by cancer, bone and nerve compression were the most common (Table 3.2). Soft tissue infiltration and visceral pains also occurred frequently. Pain caused by muscle spasm secondary to underlying bone disease occurred in 11 patients. Postoperative scar pain was the commonest pain related to treatment and constipation the most common debility-associated pain.

Twenty-seven patients recorded a total of 43 musculoskeletal pains. The most common type was myofascial. This occurred in 12 patients and accounted for 24 pains. Miscellaneous unrelated pains included tension headache, pain in one or both pinna, several abdominal complains, urinary retention, coccydynia, restless legs syndrome, and atherosclerotic claudication.

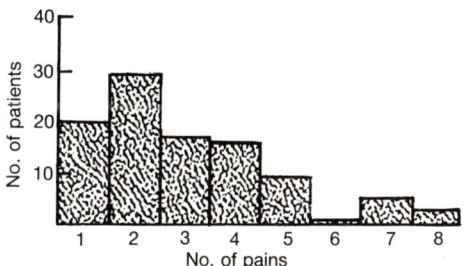

Fig. 3.2 Number of pains experienced on admission by 100 consecutive cancer patients with pain at Sir Michael Sobell House, Oxford. (From Twycross and Fairfield (1982) with permission of authors and editor of *Pain*.)

Intensity of pain

Intensity of pain is assessed both by the patient's description and also by discovering which drugs have failed to relieve, whether sleep is disturbed, and in what way activity is limited: 'How long is it since you went out?', 'What are you doing around the house?'. In addition, the patient's spouse should be interviewed; usually one finds that the patient has made light of his suffering. A patient can be in severe pain without looking distressed.

Table 3.2. Causes of pain in 100 cancer patients

Pain	No. of pains	No. of patients
Caused by cancer		
Bone	58	*31*
Nerve compression	56	*31*
Soft tissue infiltration	35	*31*
Visceral involvement	33	*31*
Muscle spasm	14	*11*
Lymphoedema	4	*3*
Raised intracranial pressure	2	*2*
Myopathy	2	*2*
	204 (67%)	*91*
Related to treatment		
Postoperative scar	8	*7*
Colostomy	2	*2*
Nerve block	2	*1*
Postoperative adhesions	1	*1*
Postradiation fibrosis	1	*1*
Oesophageal	1	*1*
	15 (5%)	*12*
Associated with debility		
Constipation	11	*11*
Capsulitis of shoulder	4	*4*
Bedsore	1	*1*
Postherpetic neuralgia	1	*1*
Pulmonary embolus	1	*1*
Penile spasm (catheter)	1	*1*
	19 (6%)	*19*
Concurrent disorders		
Musculoskeletal		
Myofascial	24	*12*
Low back	8	*8*
Spinal osteoporosis	4	*3*
Ischial tuberosity	2	*1*
Ankle	2	*1*
Traumatic	2	*1*
Sacroiliac	1	*1*
	43	*27*
Other		
Osteoarthritis	4	*3*
Migraine	2	*2*
Miscellaneous	16	*13*
	65 (22%)	*39*
Total	303 (100%)	*100*

A patient who is obviously in pain and who says or implies that 'it's all pain, doctor' is best thought of as having overwhelming pain; that is, very severe pain compounded by anxiety, possibly depression, and loss of morale. In this situation, detailed assessment is difficult. The patient should be given an appropriate dose of diazepam and morphine and reviewed two to three hours later. The probability that the initial prescription will be inadequate increases with pain intensity. Hence, patients should be reassessed within an hour or so if the pain is overwhelming, or after one or two days if it is severe or moderate. Should troublesome or unacceptable side-effects result, it may be necessary to change the treatment. In addition, relief of a major pain may allow a second, less severe pain to become apparent.

Treatment modalities

There is always more to analgesia than analgesics. To obtain the best results a multi-modality approach is generally necessary. This means using several different methods at that same time, rather than adopting a sequential pattern:

1. Modification of the pathological process.
2. Elevation of the pain threshold.
3. Interruption of pain pathways.
4. Immobilization.

Modification of the pathological process. Osseous metastasis is the main cause of pain in the majority of patients with carcinoma of the breast, bronchus, or prostate. Bone pain is also common in carcinoma of the kidney and thyroid and in multiple myeloma. Modification of the pathological process by radiation, chemotherapy, or hormone treatment should be considered, even in far-advanced cancer, although it is important to ensure that the treatment is not worse than the disease. Moreover, because androgens or oestrogens have been prescribed, this does not mean that analgesics should be withheld; a combined approach should be employed. If relief is obtained and there are no complaints of 'breakthrough' pain, the drug regimen can then be modified—a less potent preparation prescribed or the analgesic withdrawn completely.

Elevation of the pain threshold. Pain is a dual phenomenon, one part is the perception of the sensation and the other is the patient's emotional reaction to it. This means that attention must be paid to non-drug factors that modulate pain threshold, such as anxiety and depression, as well as to the correct use of analgesics and other drugs (Table 3.3). The use of analgesics is best seen as but one way—generally a powerful way—of elevating the pain threshold, though a failure to allow the patient to

42 *Symptom control*

Table 3.3. Factors affecting pain threshold

Threshold lowered	Threshold raised
Discomfort	Relief of symptoms
Insomnia	Sleep
Fatigue	Rest
Anxiety	Sympathy
Fear	Understanding
Anger	Companionship
Sadness	Diversional activity
Depression	Reduction in anxiety
Boredom	Elevation of mood
Introversion	
Mental isolation	Analgesics
Social abandonment	Anxiolytics
	Antidepressants

express his fears and anxieties can cause otherwise relievable pain to remain intractable.

Most patients fear the process of dying—'Will it hurt?', 'Will I suffocate?'—and many fear death itself. These fears tend to remain unspoken unless the patient is given the opportunity to express them. The doctor must provide time and opportunity for the patient to talk about his progress or lack of it. One group of general practitioners discovered that:

> As the doctor–patient relationship improved, many doctors found they could reduce the drugs. As the true diagnosis of the patient's pain became clear and the patient was helped to deal with the pain of dying, there was less need for sedatives, tranquillizers and analgesics. This almost certainly reflected the doctor's own feelings. Once he was able to deal with his own pain of the patient dying ... the need for drugs became less. In many instances there was, at the same time, an increased demand on the doctor's time. A number of well documented cases bear this out.   (Harte, personal communication).

Tranquillizers have only a limited place in terminal cancer care, though patients who are markedly anxious usually require a combination of a tranquillizer and an analgesic in the same way as the patient with overwhelming pain.

Interruption of pain pathways. A discussion of this aspect of cancer pain control is beyond the scope of this chapter. It should be noted, however, that analgesics alone are often effective in relieving pain due to nerve compression. If the response is poor, however, the use of dexamethasone is recommended, initially 4 mg twice a day. This reduces the degree of nerve compression by decreasing inflammatory swelling around the growth. In patients with a prognosis of only a few weeks, this may be sufficient to circumvent the need for chemical neurolysis. In those with a longer life expectancy, the pain may return as the tumour continues to grow; in these a nerve block will be required. In patients whose morale is low or precarious, it is advisable to warn that a block may become necessary in order to avoid loss of confidence should the pain return.

Immobilization. Some patients continue to experience pain on movement despite analgesics, other drugs, radiotherapy, and nerve blocks. For these patients the situation may be improved by suggesting commonsense modifications to daily activity. For example, a man may continue to struggle to stand when shaving unless the doctor suggests that sitting would be a good idea. Such a suggestion is accepted more readily if accompanied by a simple explanation of why weight bearing precipitates or exacerbates the pain. Individually designed corsets or plastic supports for patients with multiple collapsed vertebrae or Thomas splints for femoral pain are occasionally necessary to overcome intolerable pain on movement in bedridden patients.

Internal fixation or the insertion of a prosthesis should be considered if a pathological fracture of a long bone occurs, as these measures obviate the need for prolonged bed rest and pain usually is relieved. The decision whether or not to treat surgically depends on the patient's general condition; whereas in bronchial carcinoma or malignant melanoma pathological fracture often presages death, in breast cancer this is not generally so, particularly if the tumour is hormone-sensitive. The median survival after the first or only pathological fracture associated with breast cancer is about six months, with a range of two months to four years (Twycross 1977).

USE OF ANALGESICS

Persistent pain requires prophylactic (preventive) therapy

Analgesics should be given regularly and prophylactically. The aim is to titrate the dose of the analgesic against the patient's pain, gradually increasing the dose until the patient is pain-free. The next dose is given before the effect of the previous one has fully worn off—and therefore before the patient may think it necessary (Fig. 3.3). In this way it is possible to erase the memory and fear of pain.

Use oral medication whenever possible

The route of administration is a significant consideration because it has substantial impact on the patient's way of life. The patient taking oral medication is free to move around, travel as he wishes and, most

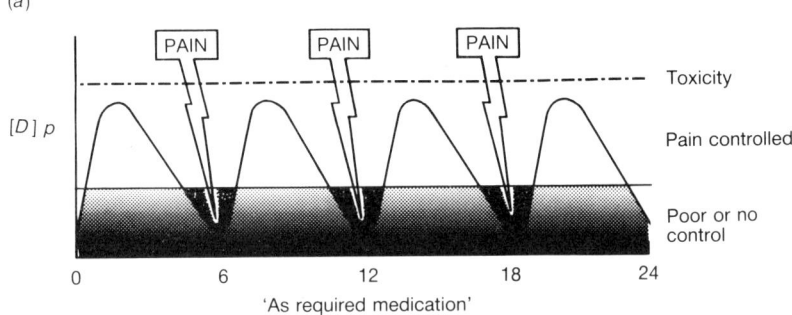

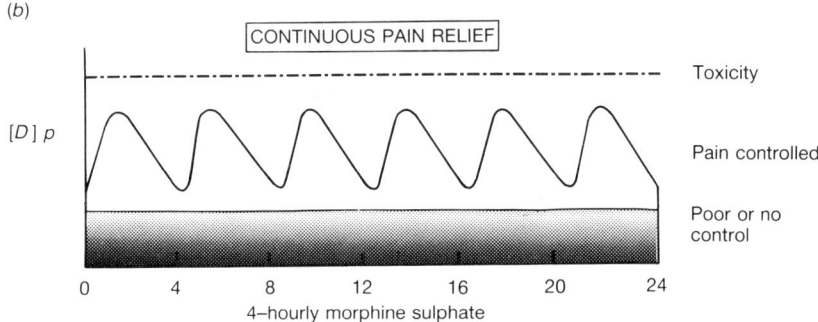

Fig. 3.3. The results of (a) 'as required medication' compared with (b) regular administration of 4-hourly morphine sulphate. $[D]_p$ = plasma concentration of drug.

important, be at home. Injections promote dependence on the person administering the drug. Oral administration eliminates muscle trauma, and enables the patient to maintain control over his own drug administration.

If a drug ceases to be effective prescribe one that is stronger

The non-narcotics, weak narcotic agonists, and narcotic agonist-antagonists all reach a plateau of maximum effect after two or three upward dose adjustments. Thus, if the upper effective dose has been reached with one of these agents, the dose should not be increased further but a stronger drug should be prescribed. On the other hand, the dose of morphine and other strong narcotic agonists can be increased almost indefinitely.

Knowledge of a drug's duration of useful effect is also important. Pethidine, for example, is effective for an average of two to three hours. Yet, it is commonly prescribed every four or six hours. This is clearly insufficient, and forces the patient to be in pain for perhaps three out of every six hours.

Doses should be determined on an individual basis

The effective analgesic dose varies considerably from patient to patient. The right dose of an analgesic is that which gives adequate relief for at least three and preferably four or more hours. 'Maximum' or 'recommended' doses, derived mainly from postoperative parenteral single-dose studies, are not applicable in cancer.

Keep it simple

The three basic analgesics are aspirin, codeine, and morphine. The rest should be considered alternatives of fashion or convenience. Appreciating this helps prevent 'kangarooing' from one analgesic to another in a desperate search for some drug that will suit the patient better. If a non-narcotic—weak narcotic preparation, such as aspirin—codeine or paracteamol—dextropropoxyphene, fails to relieve, it is usually best to move directly to a small dose of oral morphine sulphate than, for example, to prescribe dihydrocodeine.

It is necessary to be familiar with one or two alternatives for use in patients who cannot tolerate the standard preparation. Aspirin has two alternatives: paracetamol, which has no anti-inflammatory effect, is one; non-steroidal anti-inflammatory drugs as a group are the other. Which alternative is appropriate depends on whether there is a need for a peripheral anti-inflammatory effect. The individual doctor's basic analgesic ladder, with alternatives, should comprise no more than 9 or 10 drugs in total. It is better to know and understand a few drugs well than to have a passing acquaintance with the whole range. The following points should be noted:

1. With mild or moderate pain, use a non-narcotic in the first instance.
2. It may be appropriate to prescribe aspirin in addition to a narcotic, especially in patients with bone pain.
3. It is logical to combine analgesics that act via different mechanisms, for example: aspirin and paracetamol; paracetamol and codeine; aspirin and morphine. However, it is not always wise from the point of view of patient compliance, nor is it always therapeutically necessary.
4. It is pharmacological nonsense to prescribe either two weak or two strong narcotics simultaneously.
5. There is sometimes a place for a patient on a strong narcotic to have another narcotic (weak or strong) as a second, as required, analgesic for occasional troublesome pain, though generally patients should be advised to take an extra dose of their regular medication if 'breakthrough' pain occurs.

6. If one weak narcotic preparation does not control the pain, do not waste time by prescribing an alternative; move to something stronger.
7. Morphine or an alternative strong narcotic should be used when non-narcotics and weak narcotics fail to control the pain (Table 3.4).
8. 'Morpine exists to be given, not merely to be withheld'. The severity of the pain determines the choice of analgesic, not the doctor's estimate of life expectancy—which is often wrong. A patient should not be made to wait in pain until the last days or hours of life (Table 3.5).
9. Morphine may be given by mouth in a wide range of doses from as little as 2.5 mg every four hours to more than 500 mg. Only a minority of patients, however, need more than 60 mg (Fig. 3.4).
10. Injections are necessary only if there is repeated vomiting or the patient is moribund. Diamorphine is commonly used in the UK when injections are indicated: morphine by mouth 3 mg = diamorphine by mouth 2 mg = diamorphine by injection 1 mg.
11. Suppositories are a satisfactory alternative, particularly in the home. The dose of morphine by mouth and by rectum is the same.
12. Do not prescribe the narcotic agonist–antagonist buprenorphine with a narcotic agonist.
13. Preferably do not prescribe pentazocine, pethidine or dextromoramide. The first is a weak narcotic by mouth and frequently causes unpleasant mental effects. All three tend to be short-acting (two to three hours).
14. Many cancer pains respond better to the concurrent use of an analgesic and a second agent (Table 3.6).

Table 3.4. Approximate oral analgesic potency ratios

Pethidine	$\frac{1}{8}$	Dextromoramide	$(2)^2$
Dipipanone	$\frac{1}{2}$	Methadone	$(3-4)^3$
Papaveretum	$\frac{2}{3}$	Levorphanol	5
Oxycodone	1	Phenazocine	5
Morphine[1]	1	Buprenorphine	$(60-70)^4$
Diamorphine	1.5		

[1] Oral morphine 3 mg = oral diamorphine 2 mg = injected diamorphine 1 mg.

[2] Dextromoramide-single 5 mg dose is equivalent to morphine 15 mg in terms of peak effect but is generally shorter acting; overall potency ratio adjusted accordingly.

[3] Methadone-single 5 mg dose is equivalent to morphine 7.5 mg, but prolonged plasma half-life means it is several times more potent when given regularly.

[4] Buprenorphine must be taken by the buccal/sublingual route.

Use of analgesics 47

Table 3.5. Use of oral morphine sulphate

Strong narcotic of choice at most hospices.

Administer in simple aqueous solution (10 mg in 10 ml). No advantage in giving as Brompton Cocktail.

Usual starting dose 10 mg, 4 hourly.

With frail elderly patients, consider starting on a suboptimal dose so as to reduce likelihood of initial drowsiness and unsteadiness.

If changing from a strong narcotic (e.g. dextromoramide, levorphanol, methadone, buprenorphine) a much higher dose of morphine may be needed.

Adjust upwards after first dose if not more effective than previous medication.

Adjust after 24 h if pain not 90% controlled.

Two-thirds of patients are pain controlled on a dose of 30 mg or less, 4 hourly The rest need higher doses, upto 200 mg, and occasionally more.

Giving a larger dose at bedtime (1.5 or 2 × daytime dose) may enable a patient to go through the night without waking in pain.

Use co-analgesic medication as appropriate.

Either prescribe an antiemetic concurrently or supply for regular use should nausea or vomiting develop.

Prescribe laxative (e.g. co-danthramer, co-danthrusate). Adjust dose according to response. Suppositories may be necessary.

Unless carefully monitored, constipation may be more difficult to control than the pain.

Warn patient of possibility of initial drowsiness.

Write out regimen in detail with times to be taken, names of drugs and amount to be taken. Arrange for close liaison and follow-up.

For the patient who cannot cope with 'every 4 hours' or liquid medication, controlled release morphine sulphate tablets (MST-Continus 10, 30, 60, 100 mg) twice a day should be considered.

It is almost never necessary to resort to parenteral administration for pain control *per se*. If swallowing becomes very difficult or vomiting persists, give one-third of previously satisfactory dose of morphine as diamorphine hydrochloride by subcutaneous/intramuscular injection.

Suppositories of morphine sulphate are available in a range of lengths; they can also be made by any helpful pharmacist.

Other medication is often necessary

Laxatives are almost always necessary, especially with patients receiving a narcotic. About two-thirds of patients prescribed morphine or other strong narcotic need an antiemetic. If the patient is very anxious, an anxiolytic should be prescribed. If a patient remains depressed after one to two weeks of much improved pain relief, an antidepressant should be considered.

48 Symptom control

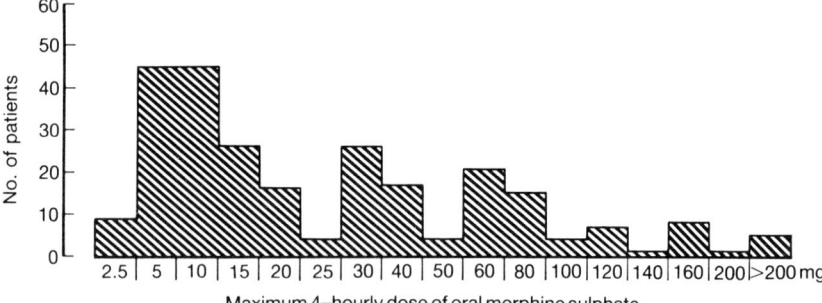

Fig. 3.4. Maximum doses or oral morphine sulphate given every 4 h to 254 cancer patients at Sir Michael Sobell House, Oxford, 1982. Median dose 15 mg; maximum 1800 mg. 67% = 30 mg; 91 ≤ 100 mg; 2 ≥ 200 mg.

Table 3.6. Co-analgesics in the relief of cancer pain

Type of pain	Co-analgesic
Bone pain	asprin 600 mg 4 hourly *or* flurbiprofen 100 mg twice a day *or* naproxen 500 mg twice a day
Raised intracranial pressure	dexamethasone 2–4 mg 3–4 times a day diuretic(?)
Nerve pressure pain	dexamethanasone 2–4 mg daily—twice a day prednisolone 5–10 mg 3 times a day
Superficial dysaesthetic pain	amitriptyline 25–100 mg at night
Intermittent stabbing pain	valproate 200 mg 2–3 times a day *or* carbamazepine 200 mg 3–4 times a day
Gastric distension pain	Asilone 10 ml p.c. and at night; metoclopramide 10 mg 4 hourly
Rectal tenesmoid pain	chlorpromazine 10–25 mg 8–4 hourly, *or* rectal belladonna alkaloids 0.2 mg[1]
Muscle spasm pain	diazepam 5 mg twice a day *or* baclofen 10 mg 3 times a day
Infected malignant ulcer	metronidazole 400 mg twice a day *or* alternative antibiotic

[1]Can be pre-injected into standard morphine suppositories (UK), or administered as B & O supprettes (USA).

Do not use mixtures routinely

At some centres, morphine is always prescribed for cancer pain with a second drug, either cocaine (a stimulant) or a phenothiazine (a tranquillizer). Sometimes both are given. Increasing the dose of morphine can be hazardous in these circumstances, if by increasing the volume of the mixture taken the dose of the adjunctive medication is increased also, regardless of need. Depending on the adjunctive drug, this can lead to agitation and restlessness or to somnolence. It is far better to give adjunctive medication separately, either as a syrup or tablet/capsule. The dose of each pharmacologically active substance can then be adjusted individually to patient need.

Insomnia must be treated vigorously

Discomfort is worse at night when the patient is alone with his pain and his fears. The cumulative effect of many sleepless, pain-filled nights is a substantial lowering of the patient's pain threshold with a concomitant increase in pain intensity. Sometimes, it is necessary to use morphine at night in patients well-controlled during the day by a weak narcotic; or to use a considerably larger dose of morphine at bedtime to relieve pains that are particularly troublesome when lying down for a prolonged period.

It is sometimes necessary to balance the degree of relief against unwanted side-effects

Examples include aspirin and gastric irritation, and morphine and gastric stasis. Generally, there are ways round these problems but occasionally a compromise is necessary.

Admission is sometimes necessary to achieve pain control

Admission brings about a change of environment. The anxieties which have escalated to intolerable levels at home, affecting adversely both patient and family, are more easily handled. The patient is surrounded by a team of people who are confident that the pain can be controlled. In specialist units, support comes from the other cancer patients who relate their own stories of much improved pain control. The patient sees other people receiving regular medication and observes that, except for the very ill, they are alert and functioning normally.

NAUSEA AND VOMITING

Vomiting occurs in about one-third of patients with terminal cancer. The treatment varies according to the underlying cause. (Fig. 3.5; Table 3.7). If related to irritation of the bowel, metoclopramide is often the best antiemetic as it enhances peristalsis in the upper gastro-intestinal tract, speeds gastric emptying and increases the tone of the lower oesophageal sphincter. For nausea or vomiting of chemical origin, (neoplastic, toxic,

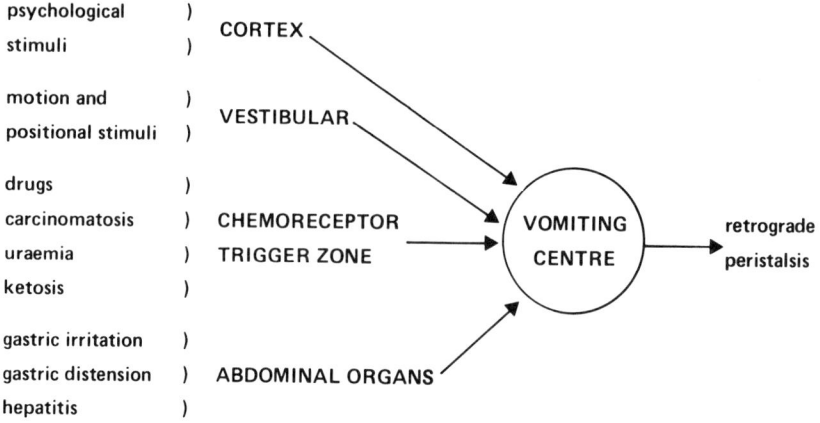

Fig. 3.5. The main mechanisms of vomiting. The chemoreceptor trigger zone and the vomiting centre are both located in the floor of the fourth ventricle.

biochemical, pharmacological, chemotherapeutic, radiotherapeutic), metoclopramide is also often efficacious. However, the anxious patient will respond better to a drug with sedative properties such as a phenothiazine, e.g. prochlorperazine or chlorpromazine. If the cause is intracranial, cyclizine is the drug of choice as this acts directly on the emetic centre. Although it acts on the integrative vomiting centre, cyclizine is of little value in radiation-induced vomiting.

At Sir Michael Sobell House haloperidol is used for drug-induced vomiting: 1.5 mg stat, and nocte thereafter. In this dose, it is non-sedative and only rarely causes dryness of the mouth. If the patient is experiencing radiation-induced vomiting, a higher dose (e.g. 1.5 mg b.i.d., 5 mg nocte) is indicated. If associated with chemotherapy, 3–5 mg, eight hourly may be necessary. In doses of 3 mg or more a day, there is a possibility of Parkinsonian side-effects. If these occur, try to reduce the dose and/or prescribe orphenadrine 50–100 mg b.i.d.

OBSTRUCTION

When the bowel is obstructed and surgery is contra-indicated, antiemetics are of relatively little value unless the vomiting is mainly due to chemical factors. Cyclizine and chlorpromazine appear to be most helpful. It is important to reduce bowel motility in order to prevent the painful peristaltic contractions which commonly precede obstructive vomiting (Table 3.8).

Unfortunately, no two obstructed patients are alike, and it is therefore necessary to consider each patient individually, weigh up the many factors relating to that patient's particular obstructive syndrome and then proceed

Table 3.7. Antiemetics in advanced cancer

Cause of nausea/vomiting	Antiemetic of choice	Comment
Drug induced		
Radiotherapy	haloperidol 1.5–5 mg at night	Side-effects rare at lower dose
Chemotherapy	or	
	prochlorperazine 5 mg 3 times a day—4 hourly	Sometimes causes dry mouth or mild drowsiness
Metabolic uraemia hypercalcaemia		
Raised intracranial pressure	cyclizine 50–100 mg 3 times a day—4 hourly	Anticholinergic side-effects May cause drowsiness
Intestinal obstruction		
Oesophageal reflux	Metoclopramide 10 mg 3 times a day—4 hourly	Do not cause anticholinergic side-effects
Delayed gastric emptying	or	
	domperidone 10–20 mg 3 times a day—4 hourly	
Gastric irritation by drug	treat gastritis change medication	Sometimes seen with NSAID and corticosteroids

Table 3.8. Medical management of bowel obstruction

Explanation and dietary advice
  small meals, less roughage
  eat earlier rather than later in day
  eat only if want to, etc.

Reduce peristalsis
  diphenoxylate   ⎫
  codeine phosphate ⎬ Choice depends on the presence or absence of background pain
  morphine sulphate ⎭

Avoid stimulant laxatives

Soften bowel contents
  docusate (Dioctyl) tablets 100 mg 2–3 times a day.

Enemas/suppositories
  e.g. every 3–4 days

Antiemetics
  cyclizine 50–100 mg 3 times a day—4 hourly
  haloperidol   ⎫ To control chemical/toxic components of emesis if
  chlorpromazine ⎭ uraemic, etc.

Trial of corticosteroids
  prednisolone 10 mg 3 times a day
  dexamethasone 4 mg twice a day

---

on the basis of 'trial and error'. If the obstruction is in the pylorus, duodenum or jejunum, it may be necessary to pass a nasogastric tube. This can be aspirated before drinks and meals and possibly left on free drainage overnight. The patient will be much relieved despite the negative fluid balance and often remains remarkably well for several days before deteriorating rapidly as a result of accumulated fluid and biochemical losses.

ANOREXIA

Anorexia may be caused by the fear of precipitating vomiting by eating; it may also be the prodome of nausea and vomiting. Careful history taking will indicate if it is the former; the latter may have to be assessed by a therapeutic trial of an antiemetic. Being offered too much or pressed to eat more by an over-anxious spouse may also provoke anorexia. Often it is possible to achieve improvement in appetite by attending to the various contributory factors. It is worth considering a seven–ten day trial of dexamethasone 2–4 mg daily. However, when close to death, giving the patient 'permission' not to eat and the family 'permission' not to force-feed is often the most appropriate form of management:

Just eat what you fancy—and not too much. Whatever you do, don't eat for Science's sake, my sake, or even your wife's sake. Trying too hard is counter productive.
Provided you are taking plenty of fluid, I shall be happy; solid food is not important for you at the moment.

One cause of anorexia is early satiation. This occurs commonly in patients with hepatomegaly and, if only to help doctor–patient communication, it has been called 'squashed stomach syndrome'.

'SQUASHED STOMACH SYNDROME'

Epigastric pain in terminal cancer may relate to gastric distension. This occurs after partial gastrectomy or with a large inoperable or recurrent intragastric neoplasm. Relative gastric distension occurs with or without gastric abnormality in patients with a grossly enlarged liver (Table 3.9). It is important to recognize the postprandial discomfort for what it is because explanation to the patient is most important, more so than with many other pains associated with cancer. Some patients, especially those with an

Table 3.9. 'Squashed stomach syndrome'

Definition
Dyspeptic symptoms associated with inability of stomach to distend normally because of hepatomegaly. Similar symptoms may be seen with carcinoma of stomach, linitis plastica, or post-gastrectomy ('small stomach syndrome').

Symptoms
1. early satiation
2. epigastric fullness
3. epigastric discomfort/pain
4. flatulence
5. hiccup
6. nausea
7. vomiting (especially postprandial)
8. heartburn

Treatment
1. explanation
2. dietary advice
3. antiflatulent (e.g. Asilone 10 ml *after meals* and at night)
4. metoclopramide (4 hourly if also receiving morphine) (or after meals and bedtime)
5. cyclizine 50–100 mg 4 hourly if occasionally also necessary

endo-oesophageal tube, also experience retrosternal pain due to acid induced oesophagitis. The aim of treatment is to prevent overdistension; this requires a combination of dietary and pharmacological measures.

Case history

A 54-year-old woman gave a six month history of increasing lower oesophageal dysphagia. Investigation confirmed a carcinoma of the fundus of the stomach with extension into the oesophagus. A Clestine tube was inserted and the patient discharged a few days later. She began to experience lower retrosternal and epigastric pain for which dihydrocodeine was prescribed. This helped a little but she then began to experience cramp-like lower abdominal pain. Ten days after commencing dihydrocodeine, she was re-admitted as an emergency because of increasing pain. The lower abdominal pain was caused by severe constipation with rectal impaction, and responded to enemas and oral laxatives. The reason for her epigastric and retrosternal pain was explained to her. Treatment was started with metoclopramide 10 mg before meals and 10 ml of postprandial Asilone, an antacid containing sodium alginate, was prescribed for use at bedtime in view of the history of nocturnal acid regurgitation and constant retrosternal discomfort. These measures relieved the pain. She learned to distinguish between gastric distension pain, for which she took an additional 10 ml of Asilone, and an intermittent epigastric pain apparently caused by the neoplasm itself and for which she took paracetamol 1g. She took this, on average, every other day.

This case history illustrates the fact that analgesics for neoplastic pain may also be necessary. It also highlights the point that some patients may need both Asilone (antacid + antiflatulent) and Gaviscon (antacid + inert gel). Gaviscon, however, requires both acid and foam to form a satisfactory 'flotation cushion' on the surface of the stomach contents. This was explained to the patient and she was instructed not to take Asilone, if at all possible, after 19.00 hours. This arrangement proved satisfactory; she no longer experienced nocturnal regurgitation and the retrosternal discomfort gradually improved. Ultimately, it becomes necessary in almost all such patients to use analgesics regularly because of the local spread of the neoplasm or gross hepatomegaly. As always, close monitoring is essential.

OBSTRUCTIVE LYMPHOEDEMA

Although relatively uncommon, obstructive lymphoedema is often ignored therapeutically by doctors. Presumably, this is because it is felt that there is nothing that can usefully be done. Progressive lymphoedema results in unsightliness, limitation of joint and limb movements, discomfort, seepage from skin breaks, ulceration, and infection. Pain is variable: in some patients the pain relates to heaviness and shoulder 'strain'. In others, generalized moderate to severe pain may occur, or a specific nerve compression pain syndrome may be present. Obstructive lymphoedema is seen most commonly after mastectomy. Extensive axillary dissection, radiotherapy, and postoperative infection are important causative factors. In the lower limb, intrapelvic disease is usually responsible.

Initial treatment consists of elevation of the foot of the bed by two to three inches if the leg is affected and, for both arm and leg, the prescription of a diuretic. After about one week, if there is little or no improvement a pneumatically operated intermitten compression sleeve (Flowpulse) is introduced (Fig. 3.6). The pressure is increased over the first few days to the maximum tolerated level. Most patients are treated for one hour twice a day. Between treatments, a shaped elastic stocking-bandage (shaped Tubigrip) is worn for as much of the 24 hours as possible. All hospices have facilities for pneumotherapy and early referral is recommended if the lymphoedema is resistant to initial measures, or gets worse.

If there is no improvement after a week, a physiotherapist commences 'effleurage', a form of deep centripetal massage. This is given either alone or in conjunction with pneumotherapy, depending on the acceptability of the latter to the patient. Some patients with oedema up to groin level, particularly if the external genitalia are affected, cannot tolerate pneumotherapy because the immediate effect is to cause more perineal and groin swelling.

Provided the treatment is carefully supervised, all patients derive benefit. In a few, complete resolution of the lymphoedema is achieved. In some, the limb size remains unchanged, but the limb feels less heavy and the range and ease of movement improves. This is the result, presumably,

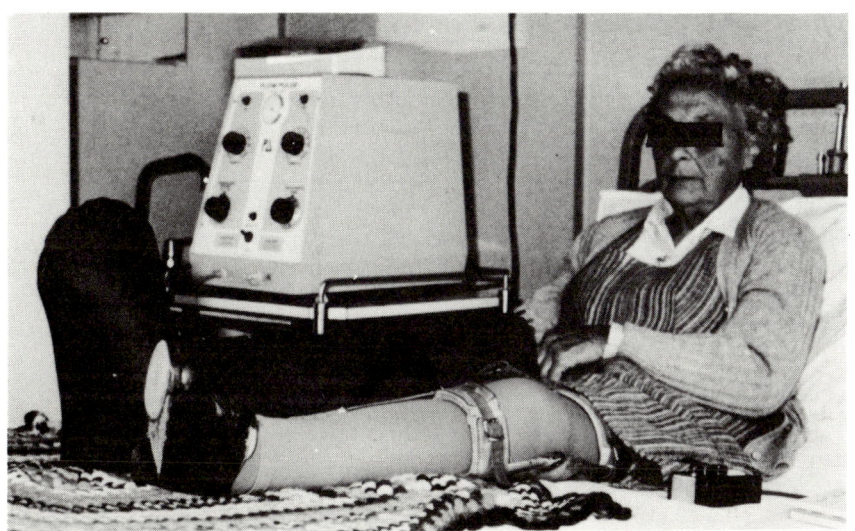

Fig. 3.6. The Flowpulse intermittent compression pump being used with a leg sleeve.

of a reduction in tissue turgor. Maintenance therapy is generally necessary. We encourage the use of a smaller, portable pump (Flowtron) in the patient's home for one hour, once or twice a day. In some patients, a less demanding schedule is adequate.

USE OF CORTICOSTEROIDS

Corticosteroids are widely used in far-advanced cancer (Table 3.10). Inclusion in this list does not imply that their use is the sole or most important treatment in these situations. It simply means that the use of a corticosteroid may be of benefit and should be considered as a treatment option to be tried alone or in association with other recognized measures. In the majority of patients with, for example, incipient paraplegia, superior vena caval obstruction or hemoptysis, a corticosteroid should be given in association with radiation therapy. Similarly, a corticosteroid is not generally the treatment of choice for malignant effusions but, where other measures have failed or seem inappropriate, it may be tried with or without a chemotherapeutic agent.

The use of a corticosteroid as a co-analgesic should be considered wherever there is a large tumour mass within a relatively confined space. There is often an oedematous area around a tumour, and pressure on neighbouring veins and lymphatics may lead to further local or regional swelling. In other words, the total tumour mass = neoplasm + surrounding

Table 3.10. Corticosteroids in terminal cancer[1]

Non-specific uses	Other specific uses
To improve appetite	Hypercalcaemia
To enhance sense of well-being	Carcinomatous neuromyopathy
To improve strength	Incipient paraplegia
To reduce sweating	Superior vena caval obstruction
	Airway obstruction
Co-analgesic	Carcinomatous lymphangitis
Raised intracranial pressure[2]	Haemoptysis
Nerve compression	Leucoerythroblastic anaemia
Spinal cord compression	Malignant effusion[2]
Hepatomegaly	Discharge from rectal tumour[3]
Head and neck tumour	Adjunct to chemotherapy
Intrapelvic tumour	
Metastatic arthralgia	

[1] Inclusion in the list does not mean that a corticosteroid is necessarily the treatment of choice.
[2] May benefit by concurrent use of a diuretic.
[3] Given rectally.

hyperemic oedema. Corticosteroids reduce this oedema, thereby reducing the total tumour mass.

The classic situation is that of headache caused by raised intracranial pressure in association with cerebral neoplasm. There may be other central nervous symptoms or signs, and patients often show improvement for weeks or months after starting treatment. When headache is the main symptom, analgesics, a diuretic, and elevating the head of the bed also may help to relieve pain. Corticosteroids also relieve the pain of nerve compression by reducing oedema of the nerve. About half of nerve compression pains respond to analgesics alone, and most of the rest to the combined use of analgesics and a corticosteroid. Only a minority of patients with nerve compression pain fail to respond to drug measures.

Metastatic arthralgia refers to the pain caused by metastatic involvement of the acetabulum or glenoid fossa. In addition to radiation therapy, maximum relief is sometimes obtained only by the combined use of a narcotic, a NSAID, and a corticosteroid. Alternatively, injections into the joint space of a long-acting preparation of either methyl-prednisolone or triamcinolone hexacetonide may be considered.

Patients with cerebral oedema usually are given 4 mg of dexamethasone three to four times a day initially. This drug is seven times more potent than prednisolone, and has less mineralocorticoid activity. No controlled comparisons, however, have been made. In other situations dexamethasone 2–4 mg daily or prednisolone 5–10 mg three times a day. The optimum dose varies from patient to patient. It is often advisable to begin with a higher dose to avoid missing a treatment effect; the dose can be adjusted downward after one or two weeks, or sooner, if unacceptable unwanted effects occur.

CONFUSION ABOUT CONFUSION

Sometimes, any sort of strange behaviour or talk in an ill patient is labelled 'confusion'. Unfortunately, once a patient is deemed confused, doctors, nurses, friends, and family all tend to shy away in embarrassment and, sometimes, in fear. Precision in assessment is necessary to enable the family and care-givers to continue to respond appropriately to the same adult who happens to be very ill and experiencing what is often only a minor disturbance of thought. Patients manifesting the following have all been reported to the author as being confused:

Not taking in what is said (deaf, anxiety, too ill to concentrate).
Forgetful (short-term memory impairment).
Disorientation for time or place.
Misperception.
Hallucination.
Muddled speech (difficulty in concentration; nominal dysphasia).

58 Symptom control

Similarly, a lack of discrimination has led the following disturbances to be labelled 'hallucinations':

Disorientation for place.
Paranoid ideas.
Misperception.
Hypnogogic hallucinations.
Hypnopompic hallucinations ('daymare').
Nightmares.

Hypnogogic and hypnopompic hallucinations are very much part of normal experience. A hypnopompic hallucination is a momentary hallucinatory extension of a dream into wakefulness. In contrast, hypnogogic hallucinations occur as a person is dropping off to sleep. In conversation with the patient or family, to call these common, normal phenomena 'hallucination' without qualification provokes anxiety. This is because of the fear surrounding the word hallucination and the common assumption that their occurrence means one is going mad/losing one's mind. On the other hand, the content of a patient's dreams may provide a useful window into the subconscious, and indicate fears about death that the patient has not yet been able to face up to at a conscious level.

CONFUSIONAL STATES

The ability of a family to cope with a death in the home depends in large measures on the doctor's ability to help patient and family understand and cope with the confusional symptoms that ultimately occur in most cases. Confusional states are characterized by 'clouding of the sensorium', are usually associated with drowsiness, and manifest as one or more of the following:

1. poor concentration,
2. impairment of recent memory,
3. disorientation,
4. misperceptions (often) ± paranoid delusions,
5. hallucinations (sometimes),
6. rambling and incoherent speech,
7. restlessness ± noisy/agressive behaviour.

Confusional states tend to be variable in degree and intensity. In the dying most are caused by multiple factors (Table 3.11). In some, symptoms are never more than mild and remain intermittent. Those associated with metabolic disturbances (renal failure, hepatic failure, intestinal obstruction) tend to be more prolonged and more marked than those associated with terminal pneumonia which by definition is self-limiting.

Table 3.11. Causative factors in confusion

1. Stimuli	7. Biochemical
unnecessary	hypercalcaemia
unfamiliar	hyponatraemia
excessive	8. Vitamin deficiency
too hot, too cold,	9. Drugs
wet, crumbs in bed,	narcotics
creases in sheets,	psychotropic
full bladder,	antiparkinsonian
constipation,	barbiturates
pain, itch	digoxin
2. Change of environment	10. Age/dementia
3. Cerebral anoxia	11. Tumour
anaemia	systemic effect
cardiac failure	cerebral involvement
hypoxia	12. Cerebro-vascular accident
4. Hypercapnia	13. Severe anxiety
5. Sepsis	14. Severe depression
6. Metabolic failure	15. Alcohol
liver	intoxication
kidney	withdrawal

Disorientation for time and, to a lesser extent, for place, is eventually the norm for the dying. Explanation and reassurance may be all that is necessary:

When someone is not well, the mind often works more slowly, and doesn't always manage to stay in gear.

Most patients are like you—they lose track of time. After all, when you are not up and about and working, time is not so important, is it?

Misperception are common too. A similar type of explanation is generally all that is necessary.

It is something we all do at times but, when you are ill, it tends to happen more often.

You are not losing your mind/going mad; this sort of thing can happen to any of us when we are poorly.

Most complaints of hallucinations, whether from the patient himself, the family or nurses, turn out in practice to be misperceptions, nightmares or vivid daydreams. It is necessary therefore to ask the patient and/or the family about the 'hallucination'. Commonly, if they are misperceptions, explanation by the doctor is all that is necessary by way of treatment. However, when these phenomena are clearly expressions of anxiety about dying and death, anxiolytic medication is often helpful, together with

60 Symptom control

continuing discussion about the experiences and possible psychological precipitating factors. Blunderbuss therapy with chlorpromazine—a common medical response to this situation—may help to suppress hallucinations but may also increase the tendency to misperceive by causing further clouding of the sensorium (Table 3.12).

Table 3.12. Treatment of confusional states

Non-drug measures

Explanation to patient, family, nurse.
Stress that patient is not going mad.
Stress that almost always there are lucid intervals.
Continue to treat as a sane, sensible adult.
Appreciate that hallucinations, nightmares and misperceptions may reflect unresolved fears and anxiety.

Drugs

Generally use drugs only if symptoms are marked, persistent and cause distress to patient and/or family. Review sooner rather than later if a sedative drug is prescribed, as may exacerbate symptoms.

Specific

reduction in present medication.
oxygen if hypoxic/cyanosed.
dexamethasone (2–4 mg 3–4 times a day) if cerebral tumour.
cerebral stimulant (*rarely* appropriate) if not agitated and if associated with drug induced drowsiness.
  (a) Cocaine 10–20 mg 4 hourly.
  (b) Dexamphetamine 2.5–5 mg daily of twice a day.
  It is usually better to modify existing medifcation.

General

  Diazepam 5–10 mg by mouth or parenterally, especially if agitated and generally restless.
  Haloperidol 1.5–5 mg by mouth or intramuscularly, especially if hallucinations and paranoia, and if diazepam fails to relieve.
  (a) Initial dose depends on previous medication, weight, age and severity of symptoms.
  (b) Subsequent doses depend on initial resonse.
  (c) Daily or twice a day maintenance doses usually adequate.
  (d) Sometimes more frequent administration is necessary.
  chlorpromazine
  promazine
  thioridazine   } Useful alternative preparations
  chlormethiazole

REFERENCES

Twycross, R. G. (1977). Care of the terminal patient. In *Breast cancer management—early and late.* (B. A. Stoll, ed.) pp. 157–63. Heinemann Medical, London.
—— and Fairfield, S. (1982). Pain in far-advanced cancer. *Pain* **14**, 303–10.

FURTHER READING

Twycross, R. G. and Lack, S. A. (1983). *Symptom control in far-advanced cancer: pain relief.* Pitman, London.
—— and —— (1984a). *Therapeutics in terminal cancer.* Pitman, London.
—— and —— (1984b). *Oral morphine in advanced cancer.* Beaconsfield Publishers.

4 Nursing care at home

Alison Charles-Edwards

GENERAL PHILOSOPHY OF CARE

Nursing the dying is invariably team-work and when it takes place in the home the team is usually led by relatives or friends, with community nursing sisters (still known by many as district nurses), auxiliary nurses, and health visitors being amongst those in supporting roles. The underlying aim is always to help people to die well, in comfort and with dignity. To achieve this end, the needs of the body, mind, and soul must all be considered. In no other area of nursing is it more important to treat the whole person. The highest standards of physical nursing care, however carefully tailored to meet the needs of the individual patient, may be achieved in vain if emotional or spiritual needs are left unheeded. It often seems easier to find time to change sheets that are not even grubby than to sit down quietly beside a frightened patient and ask 'How are you feeling today?' in a way that says that you really want to know and you are prepared to stay and listen, even if it becomes painful. The nurse should help to create an atmosphere in which adjustment to forthcoming death is encouraged and helped.

THE PATIENT AS AN INDIVIDUAL

When caring for people in their own homes, their individuality is reinforced by their environment, their possessions, their life-style, and the people close to them, avoiding the anonymity and unfamiliarity of a hospital ward and routine. When meeting a terminally ill patient for the first time, it is far more important for a nurse to get to know him a little than to spend time researching the minutiae of his medical history. As much as possible should be learnt about the patient's work, his interests and his family, but the most important information to be acquired is what the patient understands and is feeling about his illness and his situation and what specific help he desires. A physical examination to assess the condition of pressure areas, the skin, the mouth or any dressed lesions, for example, and the recording of relevant medical history and current medical details are essential, but if these can be prevented from dominating the proceedings, the patient is far more likely to feel cared for and respected and less like the 'malignant melanoma at 4 Charles Street'. The arrival of the 'nursing process' has helped to promote this more individualized approach to assessing patient's needs and planning nursing care accordingly.

EMOTIONAL SUPPORT

Not all dying patients talk openly about their situation. Whilst some are not able to, others have no one who will allow them to and yet the great majority appear to know that they are dying. This knowledge is certain to provoke some very powerful emotions. These commonly include fear, frustration, grief, and anger. Suppression of emotions as deeply painful as these will not make them disappear. If they are never allowed to surface and to hurt, they may cause or exacerbate physical ailments or emotional disturbance, such as insomnia and recurrent nightmares. It is generally easier to focus on painful thoughts and to experience the pain which they arouse when someone else is there to share it and to offer support. It is hard to stay close to someone who is expressing strong negative and painful emotions, but this is one of the nurse's most vital contributions. Some patients are able to use their families and friends for this purpose; but for those who have no one with whom they feel sufficiently secure, nurses should be willing and able to fill this role.

Occasionally, patients feel unable to talk openly to their families because they know that this would inevitably expose the relative's own distress, which seems too painful to face in addition to their own. These patients may talk to a nurse or to a friend who is not closely involved, justifying the conspiracy of silence with their relative as their way of protecting them from a potentially distressing conversation. The relative is often doing exactly the same. Sometimes there is an element of mutual pretence, both parties trying to deceive themselves that the other does not know the whole truth. Many patients gradually realize that holding back in this way does not make it easier to cope and often regret the lack of sharing. Married couples who have had previously an honest, open relationship may grow to hate the thought of their final parting being marred by deceit. Others feel they simply cannot cope with their overwhelming fears of death or bereavement without their partner's support. Whatever the reason, patients and relatives sometimes ask their nurse to help them to break through the conspiracy and facilitate open communication between them, as they have left it so long that they no longer have the courage to do it alone.

Denial, although occasionally harmful, can be a valuable defence mechanism which the dying frequently employ, particularly during the earlier stages of their illness. They may avoid any discussion about their diagnosis or prognosis, desperately trying to live a totally normal life. Even thinking about their possible or imminent death may be avoided, and hyperactivity is common. Every waking moment may be filled with activity so that there is no time for painful thoughts to surface. When denial is used most forcibly, patients may trek from one doctor to another in an attempt to procure a different medical opinion. Others will avoid further contact with their doctor and fail to attend appointments.

However openly a patient may have discussed the future on other occasions, periods of denial may still be re-entered, perhaps as the only means of defence, when the full impact of reality seems intolerable. It is only harmful when employed continuously, causing the painful feelings about dying to be suppressed. When denial is used intermittently, those supporting the patient need to be extra sensitive to his frame of mind, permitting denial one moment and supporting him to deal with his awareness of the truth the next.

This was demonstrated by a man in his early forties, the father of two young children, who was dying of a sarcoma. Whilst being helped with a bath by the district nurse, he shared some very painful feelings; grief about not being there to see his family grow up and to support them; fear about the course his illness would take and the manner of his death; guilt about leaving his wife to cope alone and anger about having his life curtailed so prematurely. The nurse encouraged this sharing and was able to talk openly about the most likely course his illness would take. He was reassured to hear from someone who had witnessed other deaths just how gentle a process it usually was and he was relieved to learn that he would not have to experience the overwhelming pain which he had anticipated. Until this occasion he had not shared these fears with anyone. He cried a great deal but was obviously embarrassed and ashamed, having been brought up in a culture where 'big boys do not cry'. The nurse constantly reassured him that it was proper, healthy response to his situation.

Five minutes later, when the crying had ceased and the nurse was just completing a dressing, the patient smiled at her and said 'You know when I'm completely better and all this is behind me, we've decided to emigrate to New Zealand. My brother-in-law lives out there and he says it's a wonderful country to bring children up in'. The nurse went along with this denial, accepting that the pain of facing up to reality twenty-four hours a day was too much to bear.

Many dying patients have disfiguring or malodorous conditions, such as a vaginal discharge from carcinoma of the endometrium, incontinence, an ileostomy or a fungating breast tumour. These people need additional assurance that they are totally accepted. The nurse's attitude is of great importance and is conveyed not only by what she says and by her facial expression, but also by the way she handles the patient as she washes him and performs other treatments. No matter how reassuring her words are, if her manner is rough or hurried, the patient will sense her disgust or dislike of touching him and his embarrassment, shame, and sense of alienation will be heightened.

The intimacy which can develop between two people when one is incapacitated by illness and the other is attempting to meet his physical needs is rarely achieved in any other aspect of care. Such a high level of safety can be experienced when being blanket bathed or having a dressing renewed, that these are the times when the most painful questions are frequently asked and the deepest fears may be shared. This places the nurse in a very privileged position, often making it far easier for her to provide the much needed emotional support than it is for other members of the caring team. The very fact that the nurse is busy 'doing something' and is not obviously giving intensive attention makes it easier for some patients to talk openly, although others are inhibited by this kind of distraction and do need the undivided attention of someone sitting quietly beside them.

Listening to patients should never be seen as a passive activity. The quality of listening which is needed demands every last drop of concentration and empathy. The district nurse who bustles in, rushes through a blanket bath and enema at a rate of knots, chattering cheerily away throughout, is saying quite clearly that she has neither the time nor the inclination to listen. But she need not worry, for few patients will force their need for emotional support on anyone who does not give clear messages of permission and encouragement to do so. The difficulty is far more likely to be in winning their trust. The nurse who appears calm and relaxed inspires trust and confidence. One of the great arts of nursing is the ability to work quickly and thoroughly, whilst appearing to have all the time in the world.

PHYSICAL ASPECTS OF NURSING CARE

The terminally ill are often emaciated, frequently bedridden for long periods due to weakness, pain or paralysis and are likely to suffer from a wide variety of symptoms, ranging from constipation to the overwhelming pain of nerve compression. Consequently, comfort is not something which can be achieved easily, and skilled, physical nursing care is of paramount importance.

The basic nursing tasks of bathing, protecting pressure areas, the care of the mouth, management of bowels, positioning in bed, movement and exercise and attention to diet and fluid intake, for example, are much the same in the care of the dying as in the care of anyone who is seriously ill. There are some conditions commonly experienced by the terminally ill, however, which require special attention.

Mouth care

The terminally ill are particularly vulnerable to oral thrush (Candidiasis), especially those who have recently received radiotherapy or chemotherapy, if they are being treated with antibiotics or steroids or if they are dehydrated. Regular mouthwashes and teeth-cleaning are the best preventive measures, but regular examinations should be performed by the nurse, using a torch and spatula. Any soreness or evidence of fungal infection should be reported to the doctor as soon as possible, so that the diagnosis can be confirmed and antifungal treatment commenced, where necessary. In order to prevent re-infection and to protect the rest of the family, especially young children, it will be necessary to use disposable plates and cutlery or to sterilize non-disposable ones by boiling and the use of Milton. Great care should also be taken to keep the patient's towels and flannels separate from those of the rest of the family, as these are great breeding grounds for fungi.

It is possible to clean a sore mouth more gently by wearing a disposable glove and wrapping a piece of gauze around the index finger. This is dipped into an appropriate solution and gently swabbed around the mouth. Patients with oral tumours, particularly following radiotherapy or surgery, may prefer to do their own mouthcare. If the mucosa is too tender for this, irrigation with normal saline at body temperature may be possible, using a syringe with a quill attachment. If this is done regularly, it may be adequate to keep the mouth moist, remove debris and prevent halitosis.

Pressure area care

Factors which predispose to pressure sores are particularly numerous in the terminally ill. These include immobility due to pain, weakness or paralysis. Unrelieved pain will often make it possible for a patient to be comfortable in only one position. With paralysis, the patient may feel sore, but he is unable to move in order to relieve the pressure. Another possible cause is anaesthesia, especially relevant as a consequence of certain nerve blocks, when deep sores can develop of which the patient is totally unaware. Other factors which predispose to pressure sores are tumours of the bone or soft tissue, incontinence, discharges from the vagina or rectum, oedema, and emaciation.

Vigorous preventive measures will need to be employed as soon as any of these factors are present. Beds should be kept free of creases and crumbs, and wet linen should be changed immediately. Frequent repositioning is the most vital single measure. Time spent explaining the need for this to patients and their relatives is time well spent, since few lay people have any understanding of what bedsores are, or how quickly they can develop.

To prevent superficial sores from occurring in patients who are severely emaciated and immobile may require hourly changes of position. If such frequent turning distresses the patient, it should be reduced to tolerable limits. In a patient with only a few days to live, dying with a superficial bedsore may well be preferable to the distress of frequent repositioning.

No nursing procedure, however important, should be performed without consulting the individual patient.

Dry skin is particularly at risk; the use of bath emollients instead of soap, plus frequent massaging with oil or lanolin, is necessary for a large number of patients. Oedematous tissue is similarly fragile and should not be rubbed. The careful manicuring of the nurses's finger nails and removal of rings and watches are vital factors in avoiding unnecessary damage.

Many aids are available to help relieve pressure. The first line of attack is usually the sheepskin undersheet, bootees, and elbow muffs. However, many patients find these hot and uncomfortable, Ripple beds and cushions are another great boon but are also rejected by some patients, who find them uncomfortable.

Encouragement to eat a high protein diet and the addition of vitamin supplements may be effective in helping to prevent sores and promote healing, but would obviously be inappropriate for the critically ill.

Spinal lesions

Secondary deposits in the spine from primary tumours of the breast and prostate are a common cause of severe back pain in the terminally ill, which is sometimes overwhelming on movement. Some patients will need to lie flat all of the time in order to keep the pain within tolerable limits. Apart from the use of drugs and nerve blocks, certain nursing procedures can also help. When turning the patient to relieve pressure, to wash his back, to evacuate the bowel or to insert a slipper bedpan, for instance, the 'log rolling' method should be used, keeping the body in a straight line all the time. At least two people should be involved whenever possible. A divided body splint may be necessary, removing the front section when the patient is lying on his back and vice versa, strapping on both sections only for turning. The new lightweight materials now available make this prospect far less daunting than a plaster of Paris cast. The loan of a hospital bed is often helpful, especially if the patient's own bed is not firm. The adjustable, hinged variety is especially useful. When the upper half of the bed is elevated to bring the patient into a sitting position, his back, shoulders, neck, and head are raised in unison, avoiding twisting or jolting the spine and keeping it fully supported throughout. The use of Entonox (50 per cent nitrous oxide and 50 per cent oxygen), more commonly known as gas and air in the midwifery world, helps some patients to cope with the pain produced when they are moved and small, portable cylinders are available.

Discharges and skin care

The frequent redressing of discharging lesions, changing of colostomy bags or perineal padding are necessary for comfort and for odour control.

Colostomy bags can be applied to many types of sinuses, in order to prevent the skin from maceration and to reduce unpleasant smells. When changing the perineal padding of a patient with a recto-vaginal fistula, for example, it is not sufficient just to renew the pad. A thorough wash with soap and water (using a bidet if one is available and the patient is strong enough to stand), followed by a perineal wash-down or vaginal douche, may be necessary three or four times daily. A barrier cream is then applied, the padding renewed and usually a clean pair of pants, nightdress, and draw sheet will be needed. The demands which this type of care makes on a family, when no free laundry service is available, sometimes results in home care becoming impossible. If the standards are lowered, the skin may become sore, the patient uncomfortable and the house may rapidly become impregnated with an intolerable odour.

Fungating tumours

Some fungating tumours are small, crusty areas, which merely need to be kept clean and dry. A little protective padding may be necessary to prevent the clothing from rubbing and damaging the surface. Unfortunately, many fungating tumours are large moist areas, with deep ulceration, local infection, offensive exudate, and capillary bleeding. They may need daily or twice daily dressings.

If bleeding is a problem, it is advisable to remove the outer layers of the dressing and then help the patient into a warm bath. The inner layers will usually soak off easily in the water. When the bath is completed, a shower attachment can be used to clean the fungating area, so long as the water pressure is kept low. The lesion must then be cleaned using an aseptic technique. The solution used will vary according to the sensitivity and cleanliness of the area. A desloughing agent may be necessary, such as Aserbine or Malatex. A pad soaked in adrenaline may be applied if bleeding occurs, or one soaked in a local anaesthetic if the ulcerated areas are painful. Deep cavities are best packed with half-strength Eusol and liquid paraffin to prevent infection and to promote granulation.

If the packing dries out and sticks before the next dressing is performed, one end of an intravenous cannula can be sited deep inside the cavity, whilst the other end is allowed to protrude through the dressing. Small quantities of Eusol and liquid paraffin can then be injected with a syringe through the cannula into the pack, two or three times daily, thus keeping it moist and preventing sticking. Raw-looking surface areas can be covered with paraffin gauze. Gauze soaked in plain yoghurt may be placed on top of the paraffin gauze or, alternatively, Bandor pads, if offensive odours are a problem. It is important to discuss the effectiveness of deodorizing agents with the patient, since their experience will be more acute and more constant than that of an observer. Several layers of padding may be necessary, and these are best kept in place with tubular elastic netting, to protect the skin from the damage of adhesive strapping as it is being constantly removed and replaced.

Management of bowels

Constipation

Constipation is very common amongst the terminally ill, largely due to the use of opiates and related drugs, the low intake of bulk food, weak, lax muscles, inactivity, and paraplegia. In addition to the regular use of aperients and, where possible, a high-fibre diet, patients known to be constipated should be consulted daily about their bowel actions and the information recorded in the nursing notes.

After three days without any bowel action at all, a rectal examination should be performed. If the rectum is full, suppositories should be given. Glycerine suppositories should not be used when the contents of the rectum are soft.

When the rectum is found to be empty, but palpation of the abdomen reveals that the colon is loaded higher up, a small, disposable, phosphate enema can be given. In order to insert this above the blockage, a suction catheter with a wide bore may need to be attached to the nozzle of the enema. If the suppositories or enemas are necessary more than once, the aperient should be increased.

All patients detest bowel treatments, particularly enemas. They should, therefore, be avoided as far as possible, and nurses must take care never to underestimate these feelings.

Faecal impaction

Patients with faecal impaction are sadly not uncommon amongst the terminally ill. Treatment may take several days. The rectum is first emptied, either with suppositories or a phosphate enema. If the faeces are too large and hard to pass, a manual removal may be necessary. Since this may be distressing and painful, it is sometimes necessary to give diazepam 10 mg orally, half an hour before the procedure to relax the muscles and to induce sedation. Once the evacuation is completed, the patient is allowed to rest until evening, when 200 ml of warm arachis oil are inserted as high into the colon as possible, with the foot of the bed elevated a few inches on blocks. There may be slight leakage overnight, so one or two incontinence sheets should be left in position. In the morning, a further rectal examination should be performed. If previous treatments have brought the softened contents of the colon down into the rectum, an enema consisting of one litre of normal saline can be given. If the rectum is empty, a high enema of Dorbanex Forte, 50 ml plus tap water, 450 ml, may be required.

It will be necessary to repeat the enema daily until a large result is obtained and no faecal mass can be felt on abdominal palpation. Aperients should have been commenced as soon as a diagnosis of impaction was made. Until these produce spontaneous bowel actions, suppositories should be given daily to prevent further impaction from developing.

The paraplegic patient

Patients with long-term paraplegia from an accident are often able to regulate spontaneous bowel actions with diet and aperients, knowing exactly when their bowels will open. Even if this is not achieved, almost all are able to perform manual removals or give themselves suppositories quite independently. The terminally ill patient who develops a paraplegia is usually different. He is generally weak and weary and rarely has the agility or the motivation to achieve this kind of independence. There are several different ways of dealing with this problem, the following being just one which has proved satisfactory for many patients. The contents of the lower bowel are allowed to become fairly firm, to reduce the risk of leakage or incontinence. If high doses of analgesia are being taken, a mild aperient may still be necessary. If the contents become too soft, a 30 mg codeine phosphate tablet may be given on alternate days. Two suppositories, one glycerine and one Dulcolax, are given after breakfast every other day. Half an hour later, the patient is lifted onto a commode or lavatory. If a bowel action does not occur, the patient is lifted back onto the bed, placed in the left lateral position and a manual removal is performed. If the rectal examination, which should always precede the insertion of the suppositories, reveals an empty rectum, a high phosphate enema may be necessary.

Fistulae

Where a recto-vaginal fistula has opened up, faeces may be passed per vagina. If the faeces are formed, the use of a tampon may help to reduce irritation and infection in the vagina and may reduce incontinence if the anal sphincter is intact.

Recto-vesical fistulae can present an enormous problem with urine pouring constantly into the rectum. A urinary catheter may help, but drainage is often impossible due to gross infection of the bladder by bacteria from the bowel. The formation of an ileal conduit may be appropriate if the patient is fit enough, but the development of such a fistula in the terminal stage of an illness can only be managed by frequent washing and padding, and with liberal use of barrier creams.

Colostomies and ileostomies

Colostomies are a common feature of terminal care, whilst ileostomies are seen only occasionally. Since the introduction of nurses specially trained in stoma care, the pre-operative and postoperative teaching and support of these patients has improved enormously. As a result, many terminally ill patients are able to continue looking after their own stomas almost until they die. Whilst such independence should be praised and encouraged, it does not mean that the nurse takes no responsibility at all. The skin around the stoma should be observed carefully. If any maceration occurs, it should be protected with a substance which will also promote healing, such as karaya gum or Stomahesive. The regularity and consistency of bowel actions should be recorded, and help may be needed in choosing an appropriate diet. A regular check should be kept on the patient's stock of appliances so that fresh supplies are re-ordered in good time. Most patients are taught to keep their colostomy bags on when bathing. However, if the motions are formed and regular, it is very beneficial for the skin around the stoma to be given a good soak occasionally.

Fear of colostomies and ileostomies prevents many people from offering to care for a relative at home. Nurses need to be sensitive to this, and they should be prepared to give time and attention to help families overcome their fears.

Anorexia

Although anorexia can be relieved in some patients by the use of antiemetics or steroids, many are left with continuing weight loss and a very limited appetite. The nurse's response must be dictated solely by the patient's views and feelings, since many will no longer have any wish to overcome their anorexia, particularly if their life expectancy is short, whilst others will demand great ingenuity and skill to help them to regain their appetite. Men seem to find it especially hard to tolerate a cachectic appearance or to accept any eating pattern other than three cooked meals a day.

Food should never be forced upon patients who are no longer concerned about their poor nutritional intake and it is even appropriate, sometimes, for the nurse to give 'permission' to stop struggling to eat unwanted food. Relatives may need to be discouraged from devoting time and energy to preparing the patient's favourite dishes in the hope that they will be tempted. If they fail to eat it the patient often feels guilty and the relative becomes angry and anxious. Only when the relative has been able to accept the inevitability of death will they have the courage to stop cooking and, instead, to spend their time just being with the dying person.

As little emphasis as possible should be given to unwelcome weight loss and bathroom scales are best kept out of sight as they can become a constant source of anxiety. If the patient is still mobile, encouragement to buy a few new items of clothing in the right size may be in order, as there can be no more painful reminder of the amount of weight loss than a pair of trousers three sizes too large.

If the patient is still anxious to regain his appetite, it is important to provide a varied diet, always served in small portions and made to look as attractive as possible. Traditional, bland invalid food can be very off-putting; kippers, bacon, and curry are often far more popular. It is sometimes helpful to supplement the diet with one of the proprietary food products.

Dysphagia

Some patients are unable to swallow solid food, but get extremely hungry. The proprietary products such as Hycal, Complan, Clinifeed, Casilan, and Build Up may be useful together with egg nogs and other milky drinks. The proprietary products are available in a variety of flavours and a choice should always be available. Naso-gastric feeding with a fine-bore tube may be useful for a small number of patients who are unable to swallow because of a bulbar palsy or a head and neck cancer, for example. This will only be suitable at an earlier stage of the illness, however, and then only if it is the patient's wish.

Liquidizers can be invaluable in preparing food at home for those who can manage puréed meals. Some patients with cancer of the oesophagus or tonsil will eat dry foods, such as toast, and clear fluids, but are unable to cope with the texture of milk puddings or porridge. Those with ulcerating tumours of the mouth may have to avoid any acidic items. Patients with oesophageal tubes *in situ* will need to avoid dry or sticky foods, and are well advised to follow each meal with a drink of soda water or ginger beer to clear the tube.

Dyspnoea

No symptom is more frightening to the patient and more distressing to his family than dyspnoea. To sit with someone fighting to breathe, whilst unable to do anything to help, is the terrible experience and haunting memory of many relatives. Remembering the high percentage of deaths from carcinoma of the bronchus and the many tumours which metastasise to the lungs, it is not suprising that dyspnoea occurs so often.

It will be necessary to spend a great deal of time rearranging pillows or lifting patients up in the bed, so that as upright a position as possible can be maintained in order to allow maximum expansion of the lungs. Some patients will prefer to be sitting in a chair most of the time, whilst those nursed in bed may be helped by a foot board or 'donkey' (a pillow wrapped in a draw-sheet which is tucked in under each side of the mattress) to prevent slipping down in the bed. Elevating the foot of the bed is also useful. Whenever possible, dyspnoeic patients should be nursed near to a window or door, to prevent feelings of suffocation and to alleviate fears of not being able to get any air. A cool, circulating atmosphere is essential, and in warm weather, fans are a great boon.

Lymphoedema

In addition to elevating swollen limbs, use can be made of compression pumps. These have boot and sleeve attachments which are pumped full of air, thus compressing the swollen limbs. The pressure can be regulated to meet the needs of the individual patient, and the pump can be used for varying periods of time, ranging from 15 minutes daily to half an hour four times a day. Used in conjunction with diuretics, dramatic improvement is sometimes obtained. Even if the size of the limb is not greatly reduced, the tissues often become far softer, and movement is less painful. Unfortunately, this is only likely to be the case if the lymphoedema is recent. If the symptom is long-standing, results are generally disappointing.

Restlessness

Relatives are often disturbed by a patient's restlessness which, like confusion, often occurs when patients are losing consciousness during the last days of life. This need not be regarded as inevitable and every effort should be made to discover the reason for it. Some of the more common causes are a full bladder, a loaded rectum, or pain. Catherization, a manual evacuation of faeces or increased analgesia should be tried accordingly.

If no obvious cause can be found, a tranquillizing drug may be necessary, but this will not obviate the need for someone to sit at the bedside. Quiet conversation and the reassurance of a hand being held may have a very calming effect. It may be necessary to place two or three sturdy armchairs at the sides of the bed to prevent the possibility of falling out when no one else is present.

If bedclothes are being continually kicked off, it is helpful to dress patients in pyjamas and cover them with a lightweight, cellular blanket which is not tucked in. This will keep them unrestricted, warm, and respectable, whilst avoiding the frustration of patient, relative, and nurse caused by constantly re-making the bed.

Confusional states

Many terminally ill patients experience some degree of confusion, although for most it is for a relatively short period before losing consciousness at the very end of their lives. Some confusional states can, if their cause is known, be relieved quite easily, and many of those which cannot be relieved are effectively treated with drugs. Those patients whose confusion cannot be cured are often greatly relieved by having the cause explained to them.

Even confirmation of a brain tumour may seem less frightening than going mad.

Every attempt should be made to avoid humiliating the demented patient by exposing his loss of memory and disorientation. Information about where he is, who he is and what time of day it is, should be given frequently in the course of conversation. The use of night lights and the removal of any objects which might be misperceived and misinterpreted as something sinister can help greatly.

It is generally not helpful to collude with a patient's confused thinking as if it were true, although there can be no hard and fast rule. It is important to keep the patient as much in touch with reality as possible. An established daily routine, with regular meal times, bath times, visitors, and bedtime, will increase the confused patient's feeling of security. Since making choices may be difficult, some decisions will have to be made on the patient's behalf, but this should be done with maximum tact and respect. People who are confused are as easily hurt as anyone else.

CARE OF RELATIVES AND CLOSE FRIENDS

In caring for the whole patient one is also caring for those people closely involved with him. Seeing that a companion or spouse is receiving the care and practical support that they need may do as much for the patient's peace of mind as any care directed at him personally.

The relationships which develop between dying patients and members of the health-care team can be deep and valuable but, in the great majority of cases, these play a subsidiary role to the relationships with family and friends. In the small hours of the night, when so many fears come out of hiding, it is the familiar presence of a trusted friend or relative that affords the greatest comfort and reassurance. Help to facilitate more open communication between the patient and his family can be one of the nurse's most important contributions.

On making a primary visit it is essential to spend some time alone with the key relative or friend. It is always useful to hear their account of the patient's condition. Such a sharing will not only be of practical value to the nurse, but it is often therapeutic for the relative. They may choose to reveal information about financial or relationship problems within the family, for example, which may have significance for the future care of the patient. Their knowledge of the patient's likes and dislikes, his special ways of relieving pain or his level of insight regarding the diagnosis and prognosis can be very helpful.

The relative may be feeling very 'emotional' during this interview and it is important, after a while, to switch the attention from the patient to the relative himself. This can be done quite simply by asking how they are feeling and whether they feel able to cope. This usually produces a flood of fears, worries, and pain and if sufficient trust has been established there will probably be a great many tears. Crying is a healthy means of venting distress and should never be discouraged, but nurses often find it difficult to sit with someone weeping for any length of time. In their desire to 'make it better' they try to soothe and subdue the tears, instead of supporting the person to 'cry it out'.

Relatives are often experiencing guilt about their lack of patience or their supposed inadequacy in caring for the patient, about their failure to notice early symptoms, such as weight loss or a breast lump, which they believe could have led to a better prognosis, or guilt about hurtful, selfish behaviour occurring throughout the whole length of the relationship. The distress may be heightened by the exhaustion of weeks without adequate sleep. It is important for the nurse to praise them repeatedly for the tremendous job that they are doing in nursing their relative and remarks about how well cared for the patient looks will means a great deal to them.

During a prolonged illness, some of the grieving which usually occurs during bereavement takes place whilst the patient is still alive. Apart from grief at the anticipated loss, there will be a great deal of anxiety about the future. How will she manage financially? How is he going to cope with their two young children as well as his job? Not every close relationship is a good and loving one, and when there has been much bitterness and pain, the combination of grief at the imminent death, and guilt about the sense of relief it brings, can be a terrible burden for anyone to carry alone.

It is important to bear in mind that the relative's feelings about his own mortality and death will have been aroused by the patient, and help may be needed for him to be able to acknowledge and express these. Simple questions, such as 'Have you ever been close to someone dying before?', or 'What worries you most about caring for your sister?', will often be all that is needed to initiate the unburdening.

It is apparent from this small selection of emotional needs, all of which are commonly experienced by relatives at such a time, that the possession of some basic counselling skills are essential in community nursing. The trust established at this first meeting is crucial, since it is likely to flavour all future interactions.

In addition to meeting the relative's need for comfort and support, it is at this early stage that he should be made aware that he is still recognized as the key member of the caring team. This will ensure that he remains closely involved and does not withdraw from the patient, feeling that he is no longer needed. The relative can so easily feel devalued when the professionals appear. He should be involved in all aspects of care and in all decisions about nursing and medical treatments with a constant sharing of information about the patient's condition.

If the patient has already begun to need constant nursing care because he is bed-ridden, incontinent or partially paralysed, for example, the relatives may need to be taught some basic skills straight away, such as pressure area care, mouthcare, how to perform a blanket-bath or the care of a catheter. The initial task of teaching relatives and the support needed to develop their confidence in the early days may make additional rather than diminished demands on the nurses. However, since they may only be there for an hour a day, the care given by relatives during the remaining 23 hours warrants the investment of both time and patience.

The sight and smell of a fungating tumour or a colostomy is repellent to everyone but how much more so to relatives who care deeply for the patient and who have never seen anything of that nature before. Before asking a relative to deal with any such treatment, they should be given clear information about it. Simple diagrams will help to show how a colostomy functions and reassurance that ulcerating malignant lesions are not contagious is almost always necessary. The nurse will then need to spend time listening to the relative's fears and answering any questions. When they seem ready, the nurse can encourage them to watch on the next few occasions when she is performing the treatment. The last step is to support the relative to change the appliance or renew the dressing themselves.

A similar pattern can be used when teaching relatives to perform other procedures, such as giving suppositories or injections. Very little information is ever understood or retained if the associated fears are not dealt with first. The distress can form a complete block to comprehension and the relative may appear stupid or uncaring.

Relatives are sometimes overwhelmed by the enormity of the task of caring for a severely debilitated, bed-ridden person, partly because they feel that there is so much for them to remember to do. They are often helped by a daily routine which the nurse can help them to plan out. This can be printed clearly on a chart (Table 4.1) and hung on the kitchen wall. It is important to group as many tasks together as possible, so that the relative feels he has some time for himself. It should be impressed on the carer that this is only a guide and they must not worry if lunch is two hours late on some days. The routine should be geared to the individual patient. The chart was planned for a patient who never settled to sleep until after midnight, but disliked being woken early.

Another area in which relatives often need guidance from the nurse is in giving the patient his medicines, particularly those prescribed for pain relief. Most strong analgesics, especially the narcotics, cause some degree of drowsiness and there is a common belief amongst the lay public (as well as amongst many doctors and nurses) that they hasten death. Because of this misconception and because of a failure to understand about the pain–fear cycle, many relatives withhold drugs until they can see that the patient is in pain, even though it has been prescribed for regular, four-hourly administration. The nurse will need to help them to understand that when severe pain is allowed to recur it will arouse fear, and that this

Table 4.1. A daily routine chart for home care of the terminally ill patient

8.00 a.m.	Offer commode; bowl for hands and face wash; mouthcare; medicines; tea
8.45 a.m.	Breakfast
Between 10.00–11.30 a.m.	District nurse (bath of top and tail; change night clothes and bed linen, if necessary; dress wound; check pressure areas; mouthcare)
12.00 a.m.	Medicines and Guinness
1.00 p.m.	Offer commode; bowl for washing hands
1.15 p.m.	Lunch
2.00 p.m.	Mouthcare; pressure area care; rest
4.00 p.m.	Offer commode; bowl for washing hands; sit out in arm chair; medicines; tea
6.00 p.m.	Offer commode; bowl for washing hands; mouthcare; pressure area care; back to bed
6.15 p.m.	High tea
8.00 p.m.	Medicines
10.00 p.m.	Offer commode; bowl for hands and face wash; pressure area care; tidy bed; renew outer layers of dressing; hot drink; mouthcare
12.00 p.m.	Medicines

fear exacerbates the pain. Consequently, the dose of the analgesic needed to relieve the pain may be higher. By withholding pain-relieving drugs in this way, addiction and escalating doses are more likely to occur, as the effect of the drug is yearned for each time the pain recurs. It is still all too common to see dying patients swinging from periods of severe pain to periods of drowsiness. Once relatives have seen how the prophylactic use of analgesics can avoid this, and have seen how the patient can be kept comfortable and reasonably alert at all times, they will usually feel able to co-operate in administering the drugs regularly.

Anxious and protective relatives will need to be discouraged from over-pampering and smothering the patient. Very few people enjoy being treated and regarded as invalids, especially when their days are numbered. To obtain the maximum quality of life, rehabilitation should be the aim of treatment until the very last lap of the disease. The housewife who is able to maintain her role by planning the meals, writing out shopping lists, organizing a family rota for cleaning, washing and ironing, even if she is not able to do any physical work herself, will feel a far greater sense of usefulness and belonging than if her role were taken away from her completely. Many household tasks, such as preparing vegetables, paying bills, or doing the mending, can be done from an armchair or even sitting up in bed.

During the last days of life, many patients feel that all they have left to offer their families is their love and their intellect. So often, in an attempt to care for the patient, relatives overprotect to the extent that the patient feels unable to give even these. Patients invariably sense when some cause for anxiety in the family is being kept from them, and they feel hurt and resentful at being excluded and prevented from contributing their support and concern. Moving the patient's bed into the living room can often help to avoid this feeling of exclusion. Although welcomed by the patient, this may be discouraged by the family, however, since the containment of the patient in an upstairs bedroom is often part of the relative's mechanism for coping. Whilst the patient is out of sight, it is possible to deny the reality of their dying and to continue living normally; if their bed is moved downstairs, the relative is constantly confronted by the pain of reality. The district nurse is often the best person to help relatives to understand how lonely and isolated the patient is feeling, to support them in looking at and dealing with their need for denial, and to help them in their adjustment if the decision to move the patient is made.

PRACTICALITIES

The practical advice and information which may be needed by the families and friends of those who are terminally ill is varied and complex. Each patient's financial situation, the existence and ages of his dependants, his housing conditions and the symptoms of his illness will create a unique set of needs. People involved in supporting these families need to regard themselves as a resource which can be drawn upon, if not for specific information and help, then at least for guidance about where it might be obtained.

Financial help

One of the greatest sources of anxiety during a prolonged illness, and also after a death, may be shortage of money. Older people, particularly, find it degrading to admit to financial difficulties, and are often reluctant to apply for the assistance to which they are entitled. The health visitor or district nurse can help greatly by raising the issue as a matter of course, in a sensitive but business-like manner. Pamphlets about the various types of benefits and allowances can be left for the family to read in privacy. On the next visit, queries may need clearing up and encouragement or help may be necessary to get the application form filled in.

More detailed advice about any of the state pensions can be obtained from the local offices of the Department of Health and Social Security (DHSS). The whereabouts of these offices and their opening hours should be known to all health-care workers. Whilst no one is expected to have detailed knowledge of all the possible benefits, each individual health visitor or district nurse should have her own collection of DHSS pamphlets for reference, and should keep this up to date by paying regular visits to the local DHSS office.

Cancer patients in financial need are eligible for help from the National Society for Cancer Relief (a national charity) with any extra costs incurred as a result of the disease. The Society does not deal directly with patients, as so many are not aware of the nature of their illness. Applications to the Society should be made by a social worker, health visitor or community nurse. Any reasonable request is considered if it is for the benefit of the patient or his immediate family during the patient's lifetime. However, all grants are subject to a strict assessment of income and savings, so that help is directed only to those people with low incomes. Anyone working with cancer patients should carrying a supply of application forms. These can be obtained from the Benefits Department of the National Society for Cancer relief (NSCR).

The social services department is the best source of help and advice in cases of financial hardship, it has discretionary powers to give immediate financial assistance to those in urgent need.

Who will help?

Amongst the health care professionals, it is the *general practitioner* and the *community nursing sister* who generally play the major role in the care of the dying. In some areas, a Macmillian nurse, founded by the NSCR, may assist the primary care team. *Health visitors* also have an important part to play if they are included by other members of the team. Where general practitioners inform their health visitors whenever a fatal diagnosis has been made, the health visitor can visit the family and offer support, often long before the community sister is needed. They will be able to clarify, repeat, and elaborate on the information given by the doctor and provide the high quality of attention needed by the patient and his family to help them in coming to terms with its implications for their future. The support of the health visitor will continue right through the bereavement period.

The health visitor may also take responsibility for liaising with other services, as and when their particular help is needed. She can advise on financial matters and may organize the provision of any equipment which is needed. She may help with all manner of individual problems and her involvement is especially valuable when young children are involved, as she may have known the family for several years. She can discuss with the parents how best to explain what is happening to the children and how best to support them. This may involve a visit to the school to make sure that their teacher is fully aware of the situation and is making the necessary allowances. If there is an elderly relative being cared for, as well as the person who is dying, the health visitor may be able to arrange a holiday admission to 'part 3' accommodation.

Nursing auxiliaries, who assist the community nursing sisters in providing basic nursing care, are often mature, approachable women. The nursing auxiliary is frequently the person that the patient and his family feel closest to and most able to confide in.

Night nurses or sitters are occasionally organized by local voluntary groups, although they may receive payment from the NSCR or other charities. For the relative who has been caring for someone both day and night for many weeks, the value of one or two nights of unbroken sleep, when they are not having to listen out for their sick relative, is enormous. In fact, this is frequently the factor which makes or breaks the possibility of home care.

Unfortunately, night-sitters are few and far between. Marie Curie Trust nurses are available to care for terminally ill patients at night in some areas, and even where they do not exist, the Trust will often pay the salary of a local nurse if one can be obtained. This is often organized through the 'nurse bank' of the district health authority.

Home helps can relieve the caring relative of many of his household chores, so that he has more time and energy to devote to the patient. They will also provide tremendous companionship and emotional support. In the case of a dying patient living alone, the home help is often the most important person involved in their care, frequently undertaking tasks far in excess of those for which she is paid. The home help organizer is always based in the local social services department. Some payment, determined by an income assessment, may be required from the family.

Referrals can be made by any member of the primary care team, by a social worker or by the patient himself.

Voluntary organizations. Many of these offer a great deal of help to the families of very ill patients. Services available from voluntary organizations vary from area to area, but the Citizen's Advice Bureau or Council of Voluntary Services will be able to give detailed, local information. Most areas have church groups or 'Good Neighbour' and 'Fish' schemes. These provide volunteers to sit with patients, enabling their relatives to have a few hours off to go shopping or to visit the hairdresser, for instance. They may also provide transport for hospital appointments or hospital visiting, or just to take the sick person out for a drive. They will usually collect prescriptions or other shopping, and if the sick person lives alone, will often prepare hot drinks and meals and even help with household chores such as laying fires and gardening.

Others who are frequently involved in caring for the dying and their families are *ministers of religion, social workers, domiciliary physiotherapists*, and occupational therapists.

Other services available

Services vary widely from area to area, but two which are particularly important are a laundry service for the incontinent and a meals-on-wheels service for patients who live alone and are no longer well enough to cook for themselves.

Another vital service is the free loan of equipment and aids. In order to keep a patient as comfortable as possible, to help him to maintain the maximum degree of independence, and to minimize the physical strain of nursing on his family, a wide variety of medical aids will be needed. The health visitor and community nurse will have detailed knowledge of what is available and will be able to match this information to their assessment of the patient's needs. If a more expert assessment is considered to be necessary, the domiciliary occupational therapist will visit and advise. Most equipment can be obtained on loan from either the community section of the health authority or the local branch of the Red Cross.

The following list indicates those items most commonly required, but many other more specific aids are available to help with particular disabilities:

1. hospital beds, back rests, bed boards, foot boards, bed cradles, bed tables, bed elevators, hoists, screens;
2. high-backed chairs, reclining chairs, wheelchairs (self-propelling or electric), foot stools;
3. ripple beds and cushions, air-rings, sheepskin sheets, bootees, elbow muffs;
4. walking frames, tripods, crutches, walking sticks;
5. bath seats, non-slip bath mats, raised lavatory seats, lavatory frames with arms, commodes, bedpans, urinals, waterproof undersheets, incontinence pants, and pads;
6. adapted feeding utensils, hand bells, long-handled shoe horns, pick-up-sticks;
7. electric fans (including those with deodorizing action), portable radios and televisions (the latter with remote control), compression pumps for swollen limbs, intercom systems, liquidizers. (Some of the items in this group are not available for loan from the health authority or Red Cross, but the local social services department can sometimes obtain them.)

CONCLUSION

When people are dying they often abandon their habitual facades, inhibitions, and barriers which we all develop as a means of self-defence, but which frequently make us appear less approachable and less attractive than we really are. This is one of the reasons why nurses often feel privileged to care for the terminally ill. It is surprising how quickly deep relationships are formed when one person is prepared to reveal their true self, allowing their vulnerability to show, and how much more likeable people are in this undefended state.

The care of the dying makes greater demands on a nurse's emotional and physical energy, her intelligence and skill than any other aspect of nursing and, in consequence perhaps, it gives rise to the greatest sense of fulfilment. The courage shown by dying patients and their relatives can be both humbling and inspiring, and it is not unusual for nurses to emerge feeling that they have received far more than they were able to give.

5 Communication

Roy Spilling

INTRODUCTION

Communication, for the purpose of this chapter, may be defined as 'the passing of a message from one person to another' (Wells 1978). It requires two participants, a sender and receiver, whose roles will be intermittently reversed. Both will bring their presuppositions into their sending and receiving, and successful communication requires that these preconceived ideas are understood by both parties.

Doctor–patient communication is a special form of person-to-person communication. Its setting is the consultation, 'the occasion when, in the intimacy of the consulting room or sick room, a person who is ill or believes himself to be ill, seeks the advice of a doctor whom he trusts' (Spence 1960). However, it is with the information received from doctors during these consultations, that patients express most dissatisfaction (Cartwright 1964; Cartwright and Anderson 1981). In the terminal care of cancer patients, these communication failures are further highlighted. Patients are slow to criticize, yet Hinton finds significant differences between their degree of satisfaction with other aspects of their care, and discussion of their condition. See Table 5.1 (Hinton 1973). Good terminal care also requires effective communication between doctor and the caring relatives. The influence of this on the patient will be determined by the existing relationships within the family.

Table 5.1. Views of 60 patients with terminal cancer on the standard of care received

	Praise	Approval	Satisfactory	Dissatisfaction	Censure
Physical treatment	12	27	18	3	0
Place of care	28	27	4	1	0
Staff	40	27	4	1	0
Discussion of condition	0	28	23	9	0

From Hinton (1973).

Communication

This chapter will, therefore, deal first with the consultation, and then consider the dying process and the special problems of communicating with dying patients. A discussion of communication within families, will conclude the chapter.

THE CONSULTATION

The last decade has witnessed numerous studies from social scientists as well as the medical profession to ascertain the variables determining the outcomes of doctor–patient communication in the consultation. David Pendleton offers a review in Pendleton and Hasler (1983), and makes a major contribution in his suggestion of a model (p. 6), to illustrate the factors operating in both doctor and patient which affect communication in the process of the consultation. This model is reproduced as Fig. 5.1. In assessing outcomes, the model makes two important points. First, there is a sequence of influences from input to the consultation to immediate then to intermediate then to long-term outcomes. Secondly, measures of immediate outcomes (satisfaction) will have a more direct relationship to the process than intermediate (compliance) or long-term (change in health status) because other influences will increasingly take effect on these

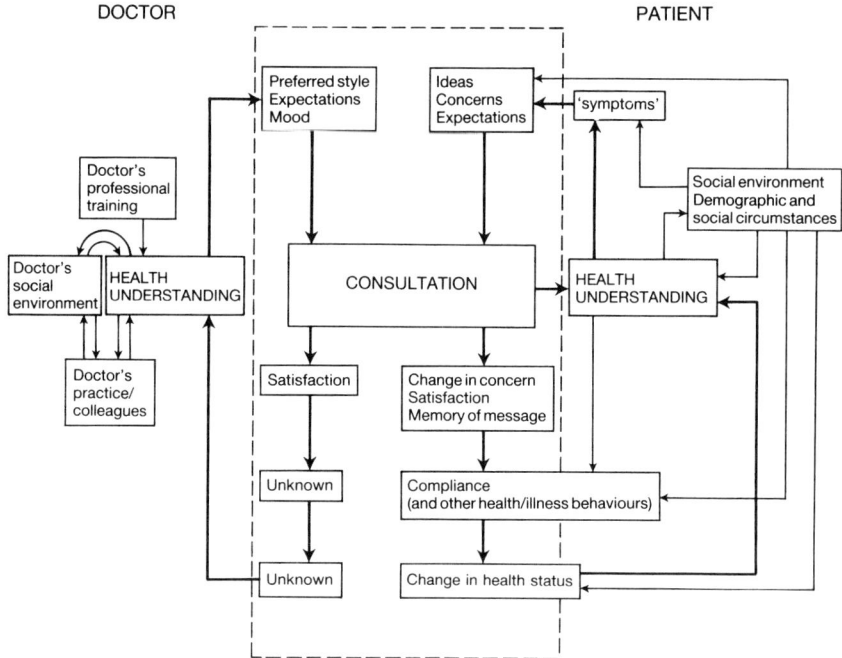

Fig. 5.1. Model illustrating factors in doctor–patient communication. (From Pendleton and Hasler 1983.)

The consultation

outcomes with the passing of time. The relevance of this model will become clear in the discussion of the dying process, where the inputs of health understanding for both the patient and the doctor, influenced as he is by his professional training, will have profound effects.

In attempting to understand the skills of good communication, the process of the consultation has been analysed in several different ways. The types of language used, and the non-verbal behaviour observed (facial expression, direction of gaze, body posture, seating position, and the use of touch) have been studied as well as the more immediately relevant verbal behaviour of both doctor and patient. Byrne and Long's (1976) substantial study of 2500 audiotaped general practitioner consultations indentified four diagnostic styles and seven prescriptive styles along a continuum from patient-centred to doctor-centred descriptions (Fig. 5.2). Although Byrne and Long made no measure of outcome, they found that negative behaviour was less frequently noticed from patient-centred doctors. In several other studies which did attempt to relate consultation method to patient satisfaction as an immediate measure of outcome, Pendleton and Hasler, (1983, p. 39) conclude that

it would seem that satisfaction of the patient is more likely when the doctor discovers and deals with the patient's concerns and expectations; when the doctor's manner communicates warmth, interest and concern about the patient; when the

Use of patient's knowledge and experience			Use of doctor's knowledge and skill
Silence Listening Reflecting	Clarifying and Interpretation	Analysing and Probing	Gathering information
Offering observation Encouraging Clarifying Reflecting Bringing patient ideas Seeking patient ideas Indicating understanding Using silence	Broad question Clarifiying Challenging Repeating for affirmation Seeking patient ideas Offering observation Concealed question Placing events Summarizing to open up	Direct question Correlational Placing events Repeating for affirmation Suggesting Offering feeling Exploring Broad question	Direct question Closed question Correlational question Placing events Summarizing to close off Suggesting Self-answering questions Reassuring Repeating for affirmation Justifying self-chastizing

Use of patient's knowledge and experience.							Use of doctor's knowledge and skill
Doctor permits patients to make decision	Doctor defines the limits and requests the patients to make decision	Doctor presents problem. Seeks suggestions and makes decisions	Doctor presents tentative decision subject to change	Doctor sells his decision to the patient	Doctor makes decision and announces it		Doctor makes decision and instructs patient

Fig. 5.2.
(From Byrne and Long 1976.)

doctor volunteers a lot of information and explains things to the patient in terms that are understood.

THE DYING PROCESS

Obtruding into the doctor–patient relationship in terminal care will come the thought of death. Using Pendleton's model (Fig. 5.1), it may seem paradoxical to call ideas of death 'health understanding', but in that death may be seen as a natural process, there must be a 'healthy' way of understanding death. It will be useful to view the process from first the patient's and then the doctor's perspective.

The patient's understanding

Age. The age of the dying person will influence understanding in four main ways:

1. The developmental process of thinking (conceptualization) during the first 10 years of life will alter children's understanding of what is happening to them. Maria Nagy (1948) illustrates this from conversations with 378 Hungarian children who represented their ideas of death to her in words and pictures. She was able to distinguish three stages:

Stage one: under five years: Death was perceived as being continuous with life in the sense '(a) death is a departure, a sleep . . . and (b) the child recognises the fact of physical death but cannot separate it from life—he considers death as gradual or temporary'.

Stage two: ages five to nine. Death was personified—either as a separate person 'The Death-Man' or as a dead person. However, she found that although death was recognized as final, this age group believed that death could be avoided by running faster than the 'death-man', locking the door, or in some way or other, eluding him.

Stage three: over nine years. Older children appeared to recognize that death was not only final but inevitable. 'It is like the withering of flowers', a 10-year-old described to Nagy.

2. Age, however, plays an important role in the creation of significant relationships, which are threatened as an individual succumbs to a terminal illness. A parent, for example, will worry about how the surviving spouse will cope, and how the children will manage. A dying parent's anxiety will focus particularly on a child of the same sex. A father will worry about his son's career development, and a mother about how her young daughter will cope with menstruation, boyfriends, marriage, and childbirth. A dying child will be most anxious to avoid separation from his parents and family.

3. A third influence of age on attitudes to death, relates to unfinished business in the mind of the patient. The adolescent or young adult finds the

prospect of death particularly hard to accept (Adams 1979). His aspirations of independence have been nipped in the bud, and his anger may turn into violent rebellion or withdrawal. Older people too, have unfinished business—a couple approaching retirement had brought the home of their dreams when the husband was told he had inoperable cancer of the lung, 'It's cruel; I'll not live long enough to enjoy it'.

4. Age also has an influence on the fear of death which as Kastenbaum and Aisenberg (1972) showed, has many different foci (see the table on p. 45, reproduced here as Table 5.2).

Table 5.2. Death-related fears: self and other

Fear	My death	Death of the other
Dying	Personal suffering Personal indignity	Vicarious suffering Vicarious disintegration
Afterlife	Punishment Rejection	Retaliation Loss of relationship
Extinction	Basic death fear Attached fears	Abandonment Vulnerability

From Kastenbaum and Aisenberg (1972).

In the elderly, only a small proportion show significant fear, and the most frequently observed attitude is one of acceptance and aquiescence. By contrast, in a comparative study between the elderly and young adults, fear of death was found to be very marked in adolescents which was all the more striking as they were afraid of very little else (Cautela and Kastenbaum 1967). One finding of interest in comparative studies was provided by the interviews of Rothstein (1967). In comparing the age groups 30–42 and 46–58, he found that older people personalize death more than younger people. He concludes: 'The individual personality learns that he will die through learning that he can become older, and through experiencing the death or debilitation of meaningful others . . . the personalization of death is similar to awareness of aging'.

Previous experience of death. For those who have witnessed unpleasant deaths of relatives, there will be particular anxiety about symptoms which distress them. These will need to be discovered and discussed.

Beliefs. The Christian tradition—the belief in both an afterlife and the perception of this life as a journey—might be expected to reduce anxiety about death. This has not been found, however, (Fiefel 1959), and it would appear that those with either strong faith, or no faith, are much less apprehensive about death than those with weaklyheld beliefs (Hinton 1963). This also seems to apply to other religious traditions.

Social environment. As Fig. 5.1 illustrates, this will effect the understanding of both doctor and patient. Communication about death is clearly influenced by our historical setting (Ariès 1976). The social convention of the comparative ease with which our grandfathers discussed death but avoided outspokeness about sex is reversed in our own generation.

Subcultures within our own society show clear differences. Asian communities in Britain, for example, tend to support dying patients at home, so that when death is expected, home deaths exceed hospital deaths.

The environment of dying patients will also affect communication. A strange enviornment with strange doctors is likely to increase anxiety; so that the patient's recall of information is likely to be less in a hospital outpatient department than in the familiar setting of a general practitioner's consulting room. Still more marked will be the difference between consultations taking place at a hospital bed, and those in a patient's own home. In a hospital setting, the increased dependence of patients will tend to elicit more authoritarian behaviour from the doctor concerned (Fig. 5.2).

The doctor's understanding

The effects of age, experience of death, belief systems, and cultural environment will be operating on the doctor in the same way that they effect the patient's understanding. The main difference in input for the doctor will be his professional training (Fig. 5.1).

Before choosing a career, the potential doctor will be subjected to a series of conflicting public expectations of his role (Kastenbaum and Aisenberg 1972, p. 215):

He should be objective and scientific. He should be warm and personal. He must exert himself with equal vigour to save all lives. He is free to be selective, to favour the 'more valuable' lives over the 'less valuable'. He is responsible only to himself, and his professional code of ethics. He is responsible to the community. He is responsible to the patient. He is a sage and all round authority in life. He is a technician, a repairman.

It may be, that together with these influences, many doctors choose their career because death itself presents a strong personal problem; by protecting others from death, he might consider himself invulnerable. If true, 'the front line of our death system would be manned by volunteers who are more intimidated by the enemy than are many of the civilians behind the lines' (Kastenbaum and Aisenberg 1972). Support for this view has come from the work of Herman Fiefel (1967). In-depth interviews were conducted with 81 physicians, and compared to interviews with 38 medical students, 92 severely ill patients, and 95 healthy normal people. He found that more of the physicians and medical students reflected on their own mortality in hearing of a death than other groups. They were also more afraid of death and the dying process than others.

Once medical training has begun, it is also possible to distinguish significant differences between the specialists. Livingston and Zimet (1965) studied 116 medical students and analysed their death anxiety and authoritarianism according to their planned career (surgery, paediatrics, and psychiatry). They found an association between high scores for authoritarianism, low death anxiety, and a choice of surgery; conversely high death anxiety, low authoritarianism, and psychiatry. A further finding was that death anxiety, but not authoritarianism, increased as the course moved from pre-clinical to the clinical stage. The surgeon would appear to fulfil most effectively our culture's tendency to remove the reality of death by making it a technical process remote from the significant process of severance of human relationships. Granted that pre-selection occurs prior to medical school, and also of the selection of speciality within, what are the experiences of death in the training itself?

In the pre-clinical stages of a traditional syllabus, much use is made of animal life and death for the purposes of teaching and research. For among medical students only 30 per cent will have experienced a death in the family, and the dissection of a corpse of a stranger provides most with their first sight of a dead body. 'The first cut through the skin is really bad; but when you get down there and it begins to look like the anatomy book, and is does not look like a human body anymore, it is not so bad' (Barton 1972). Parts that remain human, such as hands and eyes, usually prove more difficult. The post-mortem room, and autopsy of a patient known when alive, provides a further stage in the development of defence mechanisms. The scientific study of the causes of death will encourage the objective statement 'gunshot wound to the mid-brain' rather than the more meaningful, in human terms, 'His wife left him for another man'.

Thus, pre-selected and taught, most graduates of medical schools have to begin all over again to understand death in relationship terms.

PROBLEMS OF COMMUNICATING WITH THE DYING

The familiar question 'should the doctor tell? hides less elusive questions such as:

What should he tell?

How should he tell?

When should he tell?

What to tell. In his excellent chapter on therapeutic uses of truth, (in Wilkes (1982), Professor Michael Simpson begins:

> Communications, like tumours, may be benign or malignant. They may also be invasive, and the effects of bad communication with a patient may metastatise to the family. Communication may induce effects not unlike the immune responses induced by other foreign stimuli—including irritation and inflammation, resistance, and even (on occasion) shock. Like lymphocytes, 'care givers' show differentiation into killers, helpers, and supressors of response.

In a study of 200 American physicians, Oken (1961) found that 88 per cent of correspondents favoured the witholding of the diagnosis if fatality was expected. The remaining 12 per cent usually told the patient the truth, if they believed them to be intelligent and emotionally stable. It is this problem of accurately distinguishing the emotionally stable which has given rise to the policy of many units, as described for example by McIntosh (1977), of not informing the great majority of patients.

> I am sure the vast majority of patients do not want to be told what they have got. And, if we were to tell them, most of them would take it very badly, I am quite sure. Some would just go to pieces completely.... Some people will ask, though you know they are asking because they want to be told that it's not.

Yet Oken (1961) found in his study that 60 per cent of the doctors would like to be told if they themselves had cancer.

Freud (1958) noted this ambivalence in the attitude of doctors; the analyst . . .

> will no longer be able to make use of the lies and pretences which a doctor normally finds unavoidable; . . . Since we demand strict truthfulness from out patients, we jeopardise our whole authority if we let ourselves be caught out by them in a departure from the truth.

The justification for lie-telling is the suspected destruction of hope with the implied risk of decline and even suicide. Yet Hinton (1967) writes that:

> the chances are that the suicidal acts which occur in those with mortal disease are due to the suffering and spiritual isolation when the sick are lonely, rather than despair following a sympathetic discussion of their outlook.

Hope, however, has been found to thrive on information given, not witheld. Cassileth *et al.* (1980) showed that most patients prefer more information and participation in their care then they are offered. Also those who preferred active involvement in their care and as much information as possible were more helpful than those who did not. Their conclusions were:

> knowledge does not impede the application of selective denial as a protection against hopelessness . . . helping patients to become well informed does not create depression, but actually assists many patients in sustaining hopeful attitudes.

Furthermore, doctors must be faced with the expressed wish of the majority of patients (80 per cent) who would wish to be told (Gilbertsen and Wangensteen 1961). In their study, 86 per cent of patients with advanced cancer at the University Hospital of Minnesota knew the diagnosis, and were grateful. They had an opportunity to understand their illness and planned the remainder of their lives.

Communicating truthfully, 'nothing but the truth' need not involve 'the whole truth'. A doctor is not omniscient, and while he may have a reasonable suspicion that a malignant process is present, it is unnecessary and sometimes hurtful, as well as being occasionally inaccurate, to foist his own anxiety on an unwilling patient.

Distinction should also be made between diagnostic and prognostic certainty. In answer to a question like 'How long have I got doctor?', the normal distribution of survival rates even in highly accurate diagnoses will allow patients who wish to be optimistic to take comfort.

How to tell. In the setting of a general practice, it is best to allow time for patients to raise their suspicions which can then be discussed as far as they will. Most will then indicate clearly what they really wish to know. It is easier first to talk to the patient alone and leading questions can be floated.

How do you feel you are progressing?

Is your wife coping with you still being ill?

Do you have any worries?

These leads may be accepted and followed, allowing more communication about the diagnosis and prognosis. They may, however, be left. It would still be possible then, to discuss the various symptoms which might be experienced. Most people appreciate an explanation for their symptoms; others might clearly indicate that they have heard enough: 'Don't blind me with science. You're the doctor, just get on and treat me'.

The following conversation illustrates some of these points in a man presenting with a motor neuropathy associated with an oat-cell carcinoma of lung.

How are you getting on?

I'm not. I'm as weak as a kitten. Why am I getting worse all the time?

I'm afraid your nerves and muscles are not working properly.

Will they eventually recover?

I don't think so.

What is making me like this?

You have a tumour on the lung which is making your muscles weak.

Oh . . . well that's not too bad . . . I thought for a moment I had multiple sclerosis.

You may not live as long as if you had multiple sclerosis.

That doesn't matter—I don't want to linger on in a wheelchair.

It is difficult to respond to loaded questions like 'Am I going to die?' or 'Will I get better?', but these can be reflected back truthfully to find out more of the patient's real anxieties.

Communicating truthfully should be our aim, but the pace should be determined by the patient. Emily Dickinson's Poem (No. 1129 written in approximately 1868) illustrates this well.

> Tell all The Truth but Tell it slant—
> Success in Circuit lies
> Too bright for our infirm Delight
> The Truth's superb surprise
>
> As Lightning to the Children eased
> With explanation Kind
> The Truth must dazzle gradually
> Or every man be blind—
>
> (*The complete poems of Emily Dickinson.* Faber, 1975)

When to tell. As in other aspects of communication, there are no rules, only guiding principles. The main principle operating here is to respect the patient's own awareness and wishes, and to be open to truthful answers.

Most terminal illness begins with a pre-terminal phase in which the general practitioner will be establishing a diagnosis, usually with some clinical tests or referral to a specialist. Some doubt may have been expressed at this stage to the patient. It is in the follow-up of these investigations that the process of communication of bad news continues.

Doctor: I'm afraid the X-rays confirm a tumour.

Patient: Can it be removed?

Doctor: Yes, but not all of it.

Patient: What can be done then?

Doctor: We are planning to give you some radiotherapy which will stop the tumour growing, at least for the time being.

Patient: Well, that's all right then.

Few doctors would take the issue further at this stage unless given clear instructions by the patient.

It should be noted that communication occurs when subjects are avoided as much as when they are discussed. If given little information after several days of lengthy investigation in hospital, most patients would suspect the worse. Their fantasies are usually more difficult for them to accept than reality, and made more pervasive because they are not shared. Moving patients from the main ward to a side-room may imply a poor prognosis, confirmed in the mind of the patient if the regular ward round fails to call. Those dying at home may notice that visits from their general practitioner may become less frequent or more hurried, and make their own deductions.

COMMUNICATION WITHIN FAMILIES

Some doctors make it a standard practice to withold information from the patient, but to communicate freely with the next of kin. This is sometimes encouraged by relatives: 'You won't tell him doctor will you?' is a question often asked. Agreeing to such a conspiracy is to deny a patient two essentials of any consultation—truthfulness and confidentiality. It is, in effect, to deny his maturity. Informing relatives, while witholding truth from patients, would only be justifiable when dealing with children or those whose minds are incapable of grasping reality.

Working with cancer victims in San Francisco, two social workers, Barney Glaser and Anselm Strauss (1965) identified four types of awareness of dying

1. Closed awareness.
2. Suspicion awareness.
3. Mutual pretence awareness.
4. Open awareness.

In 'closed awareness' all but the patient knew the real situation. This collusion puts an intolerable strain on family relationships, and is impossible to sustain for long—particularly if the patient is at home. It leads inexorably to 'suspicion awareness' in which feelers are constantly put out by the patient in the hope of receiving more information. Both the tension and the stakes are high, and if the carers (relatives and staff) fail to respond to the cues, the impact on the patient is a vote of no confidence. Such a ploy will not only deny someone who is dying the opportunity of rounding off his business, and the support of those most meaningful to him, but also create barriers which might not have been there before. Occasionally, both patient and carers know the real situation but will act as if it were otherwise. This 'mutual pretence awareness' evokes some eloquent performances, but like Pagliacci, the real-life drama may violently break through. Only in 'open awareness' are all the actors prepared to disclose what they know or need to discover. These states of awareness are purely descriptive of what is happening at any one time, and should not be viewed necessarily as sequential. Similarly, the patient's desire to know will fluctuate, and questions are likely to be asked when doctors are not around. Close relatives are the most likely to be questioned.

Among married people who are dying, Professor John Hinton found that those who considered their marriage to exhibit a very good (73 per cent) or good (59 per cent) relationship were less inclined to disclose their awareness than those who had an average or poor relationship (92 per cent), (Hinton 1980). This may reflect the accuracy of non-verbal communication in 'very good' marriages.

The quality of the relationship will have other effects than communication of awareness. If the relationship between the living and dying was mutually exclusive, then there will be considerable anxiety as to how the survivor will cope. This may result in significant anticipatory grieving, which may require occasional support from the doctor. Alternatively, the person who is dying may represent many unfulfilled ambitions for the survivors. A son, who had been privately schooled by parents who felt an educational sense of inferiority, was dying of leukaemia; his father angrily protested 'It's not fair after all we have done for him'. Some of this anger might be directed at the patient, as if it were his fault, or at the doctor for failing to provide a cure.

Where there are strong feelings of ambivalence between the dying and his close relative or friend, violent expressions of emotion might erupt between them. In these joint consultations, doctors will often provide a medium through which these areas of unfinished emotional business can be expressed. 'I have not been able to say this to you before, because you can't stand an argument. I have never really forgiven you for having that affair...'

SOME PRACTICAL CONCLUSIONS

Effective communication with the dying takes time and is difficult to do in a routine surgery session. Patients usually find it easier to talk freely in their own homes. An unhurried visit early in the terminal illness will make caring more effective. As they have differing needs, patients and their relatives should be seen separately, however, if they express this wish, together. A frank discussion before leaving the home, will allay suspicion that truth is being witheld. The primary care team, together with the relatives, should feel free to answer questions truthfully. Nurses usually spend longer than doctors with patients.

REFERENCES

Adams, D. W. (1979). Childhood malignancy: the psychosocial care of the child and his family. Charles C. Thomas, Springfield, Illinois.

References

Ariès, P. (1976). *Western Attitudes towards death from the Middle Ages to the present*. Marion Boyars, London.

Barton, D. (1972). The need for including instruction on death and dying in the medical curriculum. *Journal of Medical Education* **47**, 169.

Byrne, P. S. and Long, B. E. L. (1976). *Doctors talking to patients*. HMSO, London.

Cartwright, A. (1964). *Human relations and hospital care*. Routledge and Kegan-Paul, London.

—— and Anderson, R. (1981). *General practice revisited*. Tavistock, London.

Cassileth, B. R., Zupkis, R. U., Saffar-Smith, K. *et al*. (1980). Information and participation preference among cancer patients. *Annuals of International Medicine* **92**, 832.

Cautela, J. R. and Kastenbaum, R. (1967). Fears and re-inforcer of young and old adults. Gerontological Society. Quoted in Kastenbaum and Aisenberg (1972) *Op. cit.*, p. 84.

Fiefel, H. (1959). *The meaning of death*. McGraw-Hill, New York.

—— (1967). *Physicians consider death*. Proceedings of the 75th Annual Convention of the American Physiological Association. Washington, D. C.

Freud, S. (1958). *The complete psychological works of S. Freud*. Standard Edition Vol. 12, p. 164, (ed. James Strachey). Hogarth Press, London.

Gilbertsen, V. A. and Wangensteen, O. H. (1961). Should the doctor tell the patient that the disease is cancer? From *The Physician and the total care of the cancer patient*. American Cancer Society, New York.

Glaser, B. G. and Strauss, A. (1966). *Awareness of dying*. Aldine, Chicago.

Hinton, J. M. (1963). The physical and mental distress of the dying. *Quarterly Journal of Medicine*, **32**, 1.

—— (1967). *Dying*. Penguin, Harmondsworth.

—— (1973). Patients views on their care during Terminal Cancer. *Proceedings of the Royal Society of Medicine* **66**, 610.

—— (1980). Whom do dying patients tell? *British Medical Journal* **281**, 1328.

Kaustenbaum, R. and Aisenberg, R. (1972). *The psychology of death*. Duckworth, London.

Livingston, P. B. and Zimet, C. N. (1965). Death, anxiety, authoritarianism, and choice of speciality in medical students. *Journal of Nervous and Mental Disease* **140**, 222–30.

McIntosh, J. (1977). *Communication and awareness in a cancer ward*. Croom Helm, London.

Nagy, M. (1948). The childs' view of death. *Journal of Genetic Psychology* **73**, 3–27.

Oken, D. (1961). What to tell cancer patients. *Journal of the American Medication Association* **175**, 1120.

Pendleton, D. and Hasler, J. (1983). *Doctor/patient communication*. Academic Press, London and New York.

Rothstein, S. H. (1967). Aging awareness and personalisation of death. Ph.D. dissertation in Chicago. Quoted by Kastenbaum and Aisenberg (1972) *op. cit.* p. 85.

Spence, J. (1960). *The purpose and practice of medicine*. Oxford University Press.

Wells, G. (1978). *How to communicate*. McGraw-Hill, London.

Wilkes, E. (ed.) (1982). *The dying patient*. MTP Press, London.

6 Hospice care

Robert Twycross

WHAT IS HOSPICE CARE?

Hospice is a programme of continuing care for terminally ill patients and their families. In practice, most of these patients have cancer. The name hospice, 'a resting place for travellers or pilgrims' was popularized by Dame Cicely Saunders, who founded St. Christopher's Hospice, London in 1967. The choice was dictated by the desire to provide a type of care which incorporated the skills of a hospital and the more leisurely hospitality and warmth of a home, 'beds without invisible parking meters beside them' (Saunders 1984). In the hospice, the centre of interest has shifted from the disease to the patient, from the pathological process to the person. The major goals of hospice care are to provide:

1. Relief for the patient from pain and other distressing symptoms.
2. Psychological care for the patient.
3. A support system to help patients live as actively as possible in the face of impending death.
4. Psychological care for the family during the illness and in bereavement.

Patients with terminal disease often need more care than those whose sickness is curable. The hospice offers intensive care for the terminally ill and professional skills of a high order in medicine and nursing are required, 'expert care that is individual to the patient, detailed, sensitive, and time consuming' (Luxton 1979). Hospice philosophy is not limited by 'the tyranny of cure', but at the same time, it is steadfastly opposed to euthanasia (Twycross 1982). The National Hospice Organization in the United States (1981) states: 'Hospice affirms life, and regards dying as a normal process. Hospice neither hastens nor postpones death'.

Hospice care is distinct from geriatric medicine or the care of the chronically sick, two specialties with which it is frequently compared.

> It contains many of the rewards of surgery, since it operates in a setting of crisis intervention; of internal medicine, since it calls for the fine titration of drug regimens against troublesome symptoms; and of psychiatry, since it deals with the anxious, the depressed and the bereaved. (Mount 1980)

It requires a comprehensive approach which considers not only physical but also psychosocial and metaphysical/spiritual issues.

VARIATIONS ON A THEME

In 1967, there were only two hospices: St. Christopher's and St. Joseph's, both in london. St. Joseph's provides the historic link with the mediaeval hospices and was the seed-bed for modern developments. It has not always been possible to build a separate institution and today a variety of approaches are evident (Fig. 6.1). Independent hospices are supported to a widely varying extent by contractual arrangements with the National Health Service (NHS). This support may be nominal or up to two-thirds of the annual running cost. Continuing Care Units are NHS hospices. These are built in association with an existing hospital, and are an integral part of the NHS. Building costs are raised by public appeal under the direction of the National Society for Cancer Relief (NSCR). These are often referred to as Macmillan Homes or Units, in memory of Douglas Macmillan, who founded the NSCR in 1911. There are 11 NHS Continuing Care Units in Britain, each with 20–25 inpatient beds. In addition, in Wales, there are eight Macmillan mini-units. Each comprises a two-bedded ward with a visitors' room attached to a community hospital.

Most hospices have several specialist community nurses (Macmillan nurses) helping to support discharged inpatients or new outpatients in their homes. These nurses are not intended to replace the district nurse or health visitor but supplement the primary care services already involved. As with

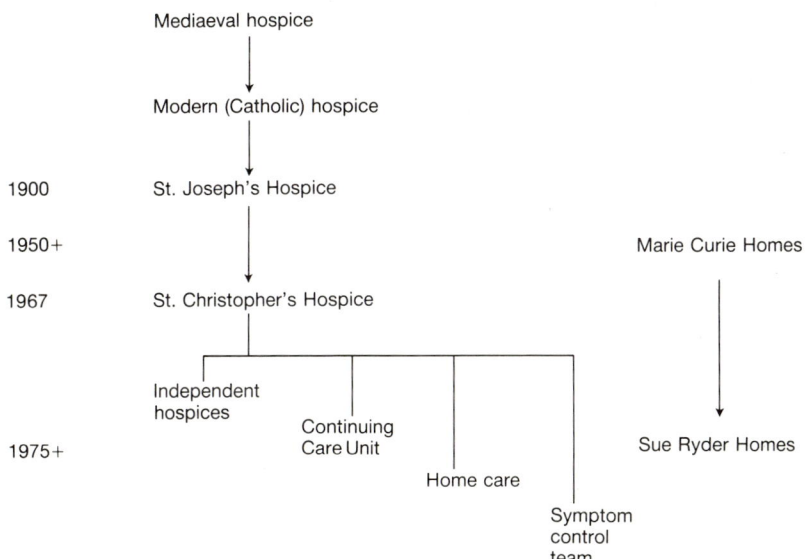

Fig. 6.1. The development of hospice care. Marie Curie and Sue Ryder Homes have less medical involvement than a hospice, and are more like nursing homes.

other specialist nurses (e.g. stoma care nurses), their knowledge is often invaluable in providing needed additional support, both psychosocial and practical. They act as 'facilitators' and can, for example, help to obtain speedily a wide variety of home aids. In some areas, they also arrange night nursing cover if that provided by the NHS, in conjunction with the Marie Curie Memorial Foundation, proves inadequate.

The specialist nurse also helps to achieve drug compliance, 'troubleshoots' in relation to unacceptable drug side-effects, and helps optimize analgesic, laxative, antiemetic, and night sedative dosage between outpatient appointments. This therapeutic activity is, in one sense, comparable to the hospital nurse's freedom to administer 'as required' drugs. Liaison with the general practitioner is clearly important, indeed imperative if the charge of 'barefoot doctor' is to be avoided. Even so, it may seem as if the hospice, through the nurse, is taking over patient care. However, outpatient hospice care may demand very intensive specialist nurse involvement if initial problems are to be overcome, symptoms controlled, and inpatient admission avoided. At other times, the specialist nurse acts simply as a consultative adviser to district nurse and/or health visitor. In addition, when appropriate, the hospice nurse offers support to families in bereavement. This is a natural and inevitable part of her total contribution.

An increasing number of hospices, particularly those within the NHS, now have facilities for day care (Wilkes *et al.* 1978). The NHS hospice will also be called upon to advise in relation to the care of patients in other wards or neighbouring hospitals. Thus the fully-fledged NHS hospice will offer:

1. Inpatient care.
2. Outpatient clinics.
3. Day care.
4. Specialist community nursing.
5. Ward consultation.
6. Domiciliary consultation.
7. Bereavement care.

Other inpatient facilities include 11 Marie Curie and six Sue Ryder Homes. Although the situation is changing, most of the Marie Curie Homes should be regarded as nursing homes for convalescing and dying cancer patients, rather than 'intensive terminal care units'. Sue Ryder Homes are best described as hybrids—a cross between a hospice and a traditional Marie Curie Home. As with the latter, however, the picture is not monochromatic, and one or two Sue Ryder Homes undoubtedly reach hospice standards.

The difference relates to staffing levels. A nursing home has relatively less medical involvement and fewer nurses than the more expensive to run hospice. A hospice, because of the better staffing levels, can cope with a higher proportion of patients with major physical and psychological symptoms, or with complex interpersonal and family problems. Teaching also forms an important part of the work of a hospice. In some, this is backed-up by research into the various aspects of hospice care.

A recent report indicated that, in Britain, there are now 64 hospices—independent or NHS, 11 Marie Curie Homes, and six Sue Ryder Homes; 81 in total (Smith 1984). There are 30 more in the planning stage. In round figures, bed numbers are as follows:

1. Independent hospices   900
2. Continuing Care Units (NSH)   300
3. Marie Curie and Sue Ryder Homes   530

Almost exactly half of the 1730 beds are funded by the NHS, either directly or contractually (Smith 1984).

In some 40 areas help is available to primary care teams via specialist community nurses (Macmillan nurses) working in groups of two or three without back-up hospice beds and often with only minimal medical support. Although obviously better than nothing, the stresses of working in this way are extremely high and, inevitably, there have been casualties Because of this, it is difficult to encourage further developments in this area. In Cornwall, however, there is a countywide Macmillan Service which provides its own internal support. Specialist medical help can be obtained, if needed, from the hospice at St. Austell.

Symptom control teams now number about 12. These may be described as a hospice team within a hospital. They have no designated beds but offer advice and support when requested by other clinicians. This approach clearly has both advantages and disadvantages compared with the original inpatient model. Scope for the teaching of junior hospital staff and nurses is considerable. It is likely that the next decade will see further growth of hospice services of this type.

Community involvement in the form of volunteer workers and fund-raising is also an integral part of hospice care. Many hospices have a full-time voluntary services co-ordinator. Volunteers help in a wide variety of ways according to individual skills and local needs. The use of volunteer workers is not just to help contain costs but to emphasize that the hospice is part of a wide caring community. Such involvements brings with it the important non-verbal message to the patients, 'You still matter to us'; and to the staff, 'You have our full and continued backing'.

EVALUATION OF HOSPICE CARE

Hospice as a programme of care for the dying has developed because of a need within the health care system. There would be no 'hospice movement' if the needs of the dying and their families had been met adequately. There is, however, still a need to evaluate hospice care (Mount and Scott 1983). Superiority of pain control when compared with normal hospital and traditional home care, has been shown in two studies (Melzack *et al*. 1976; Parkes 1979*a*) but not in a third (Kane *et al*. 1984). Increased mobility was recorded in one study (Parkes 1979*a*) but not in a second (Kane *et al*. 1984). Several studies have suggested that the patient's emotional distress, anger, and isolation is decreased by hospice care, (Mount 1976; Buckingham *et al*. 1976; Hinton 1979). A prospective case-controlled study at the Connecticut Hospice showed that hospice patients have higher levels of social adjustment and lower levels of anxiety and depression (Lack and Buckingham 1978).

Benefit to the family has also been recorded. In two controlled studies using matched pairs, hospice families reported more positive memories of the patient's terminal illness, and less severe and less prolonged manifestations of grief (Mount 1976; Parkes 1979*b*). As yet no method is available to evaluate metaphysical aspects of care. The American National Hospice Study incorporates a modified Spitzer Quality of Life Index (Greer *et al*. 1983). However, what of the dying young man who said that the last 12 months of illness had been 'the best year of my life'? On the day of this comment his Quality of Life on that index was rated only two out of a possible score of ten (Mount and Scott 1983).

No comparative studies of the psychosocial cost to hospice staff have been undertaken. Care of the dying is not easy; it is emotionally and physically demanding. 'Extremely harrowing' is how one general practitioner described it. Some have tried and failed; others have succeeded—at least for a while—but then 'burned out'. Others still soldier on, but at what cost to themselves and their families? Even from the point of view of the staff alone, evaluation of hospice care is essential. If the psychological cost to the carers is high, it could become necessary to limit full-time commitment to, say, five or 10 years.

APPROPRIATE TREATMENT

In terminal illness the primary aim is no longer to prolong life but to make the life that remains as comfortable and as meaningful as possible. Thus, what may be appropriate treatment in an acutely ill patient may be inappropriate in the dying. Cardiac resuscitation, artificial respiration, intravenous infusion, nasogastric tubes, and antibiotics are all primarily supportive measures for use in acute or acute-on-chronic illnesses to assist a patient through the initial period towards recovery of health (Fig. 6.2). To use such measures in patients who are clearly close to death and have no expectancy of a return to health is generally inappropriate (Fig. 6.3),

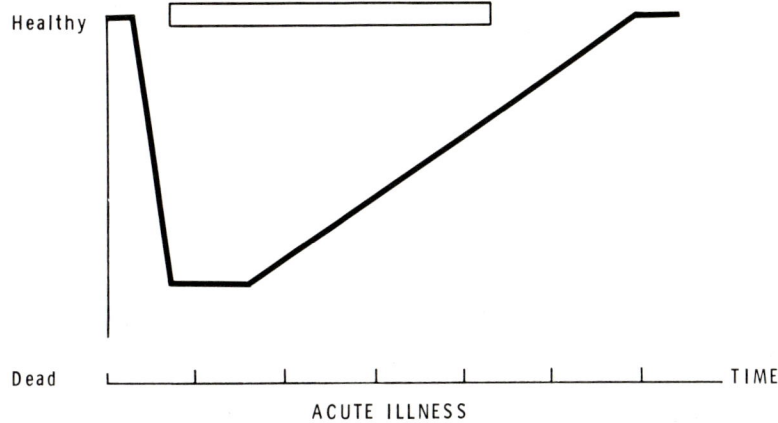

Fig. 6.2. A graphical representation of acute illness. Biological prospects are generally good. Acute resuscitative measures are important and enable the patient to survive the initial crisis. Recovery is aided by natural forces of healing, and is completed by the patient alone, independent of any continuing medical support. ☐ indicates specific medical care.

and is therefore bad medicine. We have no right or duty, legal or ethical, to prescribe a lingering death (Thompson 1984).

It is not a question of 'to treat or not to treat?' but 'what is appropriate treatment?' given the patient's biological prospects and both personal and social circumstances (Twycross 1982). Treatment remains active: 'passive

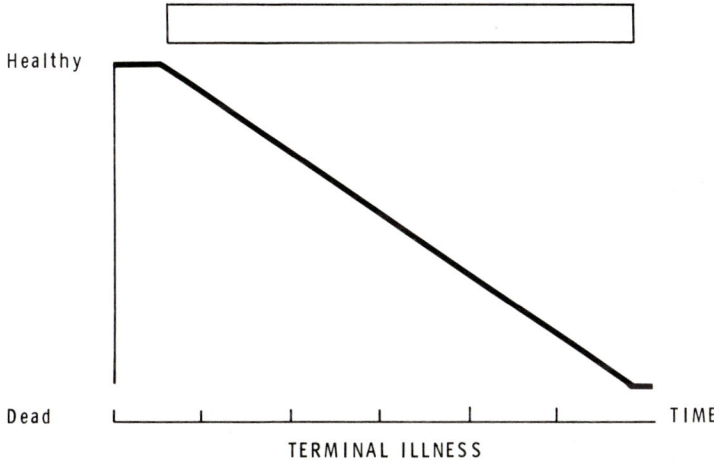

Fig. 6.3. A graphical representation of terminal illness. Biological prospects progressively worsen. Acute and terminal illness are therefore distinct pathophysiological entities. Therapeutic interventions than can best be described as prolonging the distress of dying are both futile and inappropriate. ☐ indicates specific medical care.

hospice care' is a contradiction in terms. Hospice is efficient good quality care, not just tender loving care. Occasional patients will need, and therefore will receive, a blood transfusion or, more rarely, intravenous fluids. However, for the most part, because of a short life-expectancy, such measures will be inappropriate and unnecessary.

In short, medical care is a continuum, ranging from complete cure at one end to symptom control at the other. When cure is not possible, anticancer palliation should be considered. When anticancer palliation is no longer possible, the emphasis moves to symptom control as an end in itself. Many types of treatment span the entire spectrum of care, notably radiotherapy and, to a lesser extent, chemotherapy, hormone therapy, and surgery. It is important not to pigeon-hole a particular type of treatment into a specific category, but to keep the therapeutic aim clearly in mind when employing treatment of any kind. The key points to bear in mind are therefore:

1. The patient's biological prospects.
2. The therapeutic aim of each treatment.
3. The need not to prescribe a lingering death.

On a day-to-day or week-to-week basis, it is sometimes extremely difficult, if not impossible, to give a firm prognosis even in terminal cancer. Comments such as 'It could be two weeks but, equally, it could be two months, or even more', illustrate the vagaries of prognostication. Studies have suggested that doctors tend to overestimate life expectancy in terminal cancer (Parkes 1972). On the other hand, there are many exceptions to this general rule. A significant minority of patients far outlive one's initial estimate, usually by months but occasionally by years. Moreover, it occasionally becomes apparent that the diagnosis was incorrect, and that the patient does not have cancer after all. The possibility of unexpected improvement or recovery must not be ignored. Thus, except when death is likely within a few hours or days, the potential for improvement should not be substantially lessened by the treatment prescribed.

There are, however, many occasions when it is appropriate to 'give death a chance'. All our patients *must* die eventually: ultimately nature will take its course. The art of medicine, in this respect, is to decide when life sustenance is essentially futile and, therefore, when to allow death to occur without further impediment. Antibiotics are often appropriate for the patient with lung cancer who develops a chest infection while he is still up and about, independent and has relatively minor symptoms. On the other hand, pneumonia should still be 'the old man's friend' and, particularly if the burden of living is considerable, it might be more appropriate not to use antibiotics, at least initially. When it is difficult to make a decision, the 'two-day rule' should be invoked: if the patient is clearly holding his own after two days of straightforward symptom relief, prescribe antibiotics. If he is clearly much worse do not.

The use of dexamethasone in brain tumours may also cause difficulties when the patient is near to death. Here it is important to recall the original therapeutic aim: the remission of neurological symptoms with a view to partial or complete physical rehabilitation. With continued tumour growth, the benefits won with the corticosteroids will be lost progressively. When the patient is more or less bed-ridden, hemiplegic, drowsy, dysphasic, intermittently confused, incontinent, and requiring more than one person to help change his position, the rehabilitative role of the corticosteroid has clearly ceased. In these circumstances, the continued use of dexamethasone has become the prescription of a lingering death. Stopping the corticosteroid, however, may present a tactical dilemma, although not an ethical one. This is because, at the time of initial prescription, the patient and his family received the message (either verbal or non-verbal): 'Be sure to take these tablets. You will die/get rapidly worse without them'. And even when close to death, the emotions of the patient and close relatives often remain surprisingly ambivalent. Sometimes it is necessary to admit to hospital to allow staff-controlled dose reduction. Ideally it should be possible to say:

These tablets were to help keep you on your feet (etc.) and are now quite clearly not able to achieve their aim. Tablets which have served their purpose are best stopped. I suggest we stop the second dose today and halve the early morning one tomorrow. I will look in again the day after tomorrow to review things. If there is cause for concern between now and then, please ring the surgery and ask to speak to me. In any case, the district nurse will be in twice a day as usual—and she knows how to track me down.

It must be emphasized that cessation of corticosteroid treatment is a medicial decision—to be taken by the doctor. It is quite wrong, in the author's opinion, to ask the family to decide. To do so suggests that the doctor is not sure of the ethical ground on which he is standing.

On many occasions, as patients become bed-ridden, it is sensible to phase out the less important medications. Iron, multivitamins, potassium, digoxin are all long-term supportive treatments and are irrelevant when the patient is close to death. Hypotensives can often be phased out early on as weight loss and/or other medication (e.g. morphine, diazepam) alter the patient's need. Continuation of pre-existing diuretic therapy may cause postural hypotension and gross debility unless the dose is reduced or temporarily stopped in the face of a poor fluid intake or repeated vomiting. For the patient who is very attached to certain long-standing treatments the concept of temporary cessation with early review after three for four days should be invoked. This avoids putting the patient in a mental cul-de-sac, and also gives maximum room for manoeuvre on the doctor's part. Being sensitive to the patient's sensibilities is part of good terminal care.

REHABILITATION

Rehabilitation may be defined as the treatment and training of disabled individuals to enable them to achieve their maximum potential for normal living, physically, emotionally, socially, and vocationally. Rehabilitation is an integral part of hospice care. Although eventually physical rehabilitation becomes impossible, many terminally ill patients are unnecessarily restricted, often by relatives, even when capable of a greater degree of activity and independence. A patient's potential will be realized, however, only if troublesome symptoms are controlled and gentle encouragement is given by an attentive doctor.

It is important, therefore, not to assume automatically that a sudden deterioration or change relates to the inexorable progression of the disease. Is the patient exhausted because of sleepless, pain-filled nights? Has he caught flu from another member of the family or a friend? Is he the only person with gastro-intestinal symptoms—or is it an attack of 'D and V'? The list of possible causes of deterioration is endless. What is needed is not a check-list but an awareness of the fact that a significant number of patients are forced prematurely into a dying role because the portents are misread. After an 'open and shut' laparotomy, it is important to encourage normal, even if slow, postoperative care. Although, of course, if very ill beforehand, the patient may never recuperate after such an operation.

Many general practitioners still do not appreciate the opportunities that exist for rehabilitation in terminal cancer. This stems partly from relative inexperience in terminal cancer care but possibly also relates to over-negative attitudes towards cancer. It *is* possible to live for five or more years with bone secondaries from breast cancer. Stilboestrol can radically alter prognosis in the patient with newly diagnosed disseminated prostatic carcinoma. The median survival after diagnosis of carcinoma of the pancreas may be less than six months but this means that half the patients live longer, and a few much longer. Furthermore, symptom relief alone often achieves considerable short-term improvement.

In many hospices, 25–40 per cent of first admissions result in discharge. This illustrates that the hospice goal 'to provide a support system to help patients live as actively as possible in the face of impending death' is not hollow sentiment or extravagant window-dressing. The concept of living with cancer—until death comes—is still foreign to many patients, their families and, regrettably, to many doctors and nurses as well. Cancer is a spectrum of disorders and, even when incurable, rates of progression vary widely. Not infrequently, I stress 'You appear to have a grumbling cancer' and proceed to encourage a more positive outlook and life-style. One of the ways a hospice can help primary care is to offer assessment admissions with a view to rehabilitation. The general practitioner suspects under-performance stemming from an over-negative attitude in the patient to cancer. Encouragement at home has failed to make any difference. In this circumstance, attendance at a hospice day unit alone may make a big difference. Inpatient admission is sometimes necessary though to overcome the accumulated negativity. The key to successful rehabilitation is inevitably in the patient's mind more than in the body.

A word of warning: not all hospices adopt a truly rehabilitative approach to patient care. The principle of 'no bedside parking meter' is not sufficiently balanced by the parallel principle of 'living with terminal cancer'. Or perhaps it is a case of concentrating on psychological rehabilitation (acceptance of diagnosis and probable short prognosis) at the expense of the physical. On this basis, it is possible to categorize hospices into two types: those that adopt a 'cocoon' approach and those which prefer the 'cradle'. The cocoon provides a total sanctuary for the patient; admissions tend to be longer and discharges fewer. In contrast, the cradle invites progression towards independence.

HOPE

Hope may be defined as an expectation greater than zero of achieving a desired goal. It is a much broader phenomenon than mere hope of recovery. Hope tends to diminish when the patient is mentally isolated by a 'conspiracy of silence'; when it is implied 'there is nothing more than can be done'; when pain and other symptoms remain unrelieved or ignored; and when the patient feels alone or unsupported.

'Never destroy hope' is frequently used as a reason for not informing a patient of the seriousness of his situation. However, glib, false optimism is a potent destroyer of hope. On the other hand, an unwise catharsis by the doctor of all that is negative, either to the patient or to the family, may make the doctor feel easier but it can irreversibly destroy hope and result in intractable anxiety and despair. Again, it is necessary to seek to apply two parallel principles. The first 'Never lie to a patient', and the second 'Avoid total candour'. Human beings—patients and doctors included—are best served when realism is tinged with optimism. Gentle, sympathetic, and gradual communication of the truth, within the context of continued support and encouragement, almost always restores hope. It only does so, however, if the patient has a goal at which to aim and a direction in which to move. Hospice care restores hope by giving the patient direction and by encouraging realistic goals. Telling the patient what you plan to do about his pain and other symptoms gives direction, and helps to counter the living nightmare of never-ending unendurable pain or other physical distress.

In short, communication of painful truth does not equal destruction of hope. Despite continued physical deterioration, hope can be renewed when the patient is helped to face up to the diagnosis and prognosis. Hope of recovery is replaced by the more diffuse hope of a peaceful death, hope that one's life has been worthwhile, and the hope of immortality in some form.

PROFESSIONAL FRIENDSHIP

The fear has been expressed that hospice care could become just one more 'technique' within contemporary high-technology mainstream medicine (O'Donovan 1982). A technique behind which professionals could hide and through which they could soullessly exercise 'power'. This danger can be avoided, provided hospice care continues to mean companionship—the friendship of professional staff with those who are dying.

In a crisis we all need friends. When dying we need a friend who can explain why there is pain, or shortness of breath, or constipation, or weakness, and so on. Someone who can explain what is happening in simple terms. Explanation is a key modality of treatment; it cuts the illness and the symptoms down in size psychologically. The situation is no longer shrouded in total mystery as there is someone who can explain what is going on. This is reassuring.

People sometimes comment: 'I suppose you become hardened to it in time and develop a protective shell'. The answer to that is an emphatic 'No.'. Obviously, one becomes more familiar with the many and varied practical challenges of terminal illness, and one acquires a certain confidence from this. However this is not the same as becoming hardened. For me, the opposite is true; I feel more vulnerable as each year passes. Terminal care is, and always will be, extremely demanding of the carers' emotional resources. It is hard to tell a patient: 'Yes it is a cancer', or 'Yes, the illness does seem to be winning'. It is especially hard if the patient is 16 or 26, although even at 76 or 86 it is not easy. Indeed, if ever it seems easy, a doctor can be sure that he is no longer of much use to his patients (Twycross 1984).

CARE OF THE WHOLE PERSON

As already emphasized a hospice seeks to offer 'whole-person care'. The staff aim to help the patient do his best given his personality, his family, his cultural background, his beliefs, his age, his illness, his symptoms, his anxieties, and his fears. There is need for flexibility. There is also a need to prevent that flexibility becoming an alternative rigidity. Unfortunately, this is an ever-present danger as corporate man tends to take refuge in the 'comfort' of rules, regulations, and routines. A freedom to invite patients to use first names can become oppressive if taken for granted. It is important to meet patients where they are psychologically and as they are physically and culturally. There is no such creature as the typical dying patient.

Body, mind, spirit, and family relationships are all important. The patient and his family is the unit of care. There is much written about the physical and emotional needs of the dying (Kubler-Ross 1970; Stedeford 1984); far less about spiritual care. Although perhaps harder to define and describe, the spiritual aspects of care are obviously important. In considering these, it is necessary to begin by asserting the obvious, namely, that man is a spiritual animal (Hardy 1979). Human life is not simply governed by instinct and hormones. Human desire extends beyond the more fundamental appetites of food, comfort, and sex. Man is a questioning and questing creature: 'Why, why, why? Particularly when serious illness strikes, there is need to reflect on meaning and purpose in life. When newly-released from concentration camp, Frankl (1963) wrote:

Another time we were at work in a trench. The dawn was gray around us; gray was the sky above; gray the snow in the pale light of dawn; gray the rags in which my fellow prisoners were clad, and gray their faces ... I was struggling to find the reason for my sufferings, my slow dying. In a last violent protest against the hopelessness of imminent death, I sensed my spirit piercing through the enveloping gloom. I felt it transcend that hopeless, meaningless world and from somewhere I heard a victorious 'Yes' in answer to my question of the existence of an ultimate purpose. At that moment a light was lit in a distant farmhouse, which stood on the horizon as if painted there, in the midst of the miserable gray of a dawning morning in Bavaria. *Et lux in tenebris lucet*—and the light shineth in the darkness.

Frankl also emphasizes that it is a peculiarity of man that he can live only by looking to the future—*sub specie aeternitatis*. Moreover:

'If there is a meaning in life at all, then there must be a meaning in suffering. Suffering is an ineradicable part of life, even as fate and death. Without suffering and human death, life cannot be complete'.

And as Nietzsche said: 'He who has a why to live can bear almost any how'.

The modern hospice is rooted in Christian philosophy, although in practice it is more broadly theistic. Those who work with the dying must believe in life, must believe that life is not just by chance but by design, and if design, then Designer. This is true whether expressed or not. Life is seen as having meaning and purpose throughout the period of dying. This conviction is manifested by attitudes and deeds rather than with words, and in how we respond to the dying and care for them, far more than in what we say. As always: actions speak louder than words. The unspoken message has been succinctly summarized by the founder of St. Christopher's Hospice, Dame Cicely Saunders:

'You matter because you are you. You matter to the last moment of your life, and we will do all we can not only to help you die peacefully, but to live until you die'.

It is this unspoken message that brings a sense of security to those cared for. As many patients have said: 'It is wonderful to feel safe again'. This security enables the individual patient to consider within himself those fundamental questions concerning life, God, and the hereafter. Such contemplation is greatly facilitated by the physical comfort for which hospices have rightly become noted. Spiritual care is therefore basically non-verbal, but none the less real for that.

When dying, many people take stock of their lives for the first time:

I have lived a good life.
I never did anyone any harm.
Why did it happen to me?

Only a minority of patients discuss these metaphysical aspects of life and death with their doctor, although the majority do so with the nurses, social worker, or with relatives and close friends. It is important to recognize that the dying to consider such issues and be able to respond sympathetically if a patient chooses to raise them.

Patients are very perceptive, and they are unlikely to embarrass a doctor if they sense that communication at this level will cause discomfort. The doctor's primary responsibility is to help maintain an environment which is supportive of the patient. This requires control of symptoms so that the patient is able to consider these issues. When possible and appropriate, it is right for the doctor to alert the chaplain, priest or rabbi to the fact that 'Mr Smith is seriously ill and may appreciate a visit'. Although regard for the patient as an individual does not allow the imposition of one's own beliefs, it is important to appreciate that many patients are comforted by the discovery that their doctor has a religious faith.

All hospices have a chaplain or chaplains, mostly part-time. National Health service hospices have, of course, the services of the Hospital Chaplaincy. The patients own clergy are also welcome visitors. Together this provides one-to-one pastoral care as needed. At Sir Michael Sobell House formal religious services are held twice a week for those who wish to attend.

TEAM-WORK

The needs of the dying patient are considerable (Table 6.1). When considered as a whole, it is quite apparent that terminal care cannot be administered by any one individual, only by a group of individuals working together as a team. The composition of the team may vary but includes the patient himself, the immediate family, friends, doctor(s), nurses, social worker, therapists, priest and, on occasion, lawyer. The team is collectively concerned for the total well-being of the patient and the family—physical,

Table 6.1. The needs of the dying patient

Physiological	Good symptom control
Safety	A feeling of security
Belonging	The need to be needed; the need *not* to feel a burden
Love	Expressions of affection; human contact (touch)
Understanding	Explanation about symptoms and the disease
	Opportunity to discuss the process of dying
Acceptance	Regardless of mood and sociability
Self-esteem	Involve in decision making, particularly as physical dependency on others increase
	The opportunity to give as well as to receive

psychological, spiritual, and social. In this situation, roles may become blurred, at least at the edges. Moreover, unless the nurses, and at home the family, actively participate in symptom control, the lead given by the doctor will be seriously undermined. Indeed for every step forward there may be a step backwards unless the nurses:

1. Give the patient opportunity to express anxieties and fears.
2. Encourage the patient by quietly emphasizing that his symptom(s) will soon be better controlled.
3. Advise about diet and fluid intake.
4. Contact the doctor if the patient fails to get a good night's sleep.
5. Contact the doctor rather than wait for his next visit or round if the patient becomes less well when a new treatment is started.
6. Advise the patient when to increase the dose of analgesic.
7. Support the patient through the period of initial side-effects commonly seen with morphine-like drugs.

Without this degree of involvement, the doctor's task is made considerably more difficult and, occasionally, impossible. On the other hand, a nurse is unlikely to feel happy involving herself in these ways unless she is encouraged to by the doctor. Moreover, how can a nurse raise expectations concerning comfort if the doctor is disinterested or inept? It is necessary, therefore, for doctors and nurses to establish a common baseline of intent in relation to the terminally ill. From this foundation, enriched by mutual trust and respect, the possibility of good terminal care emerges.

ARE HOSPICES REALLY NECESSARY?

All that has been said about hospice care is theoretically also true of primary care. After all, for example, the general practitioner is concerned about the whole person, and looks on the patient and his family as the unit of care. However, there are few general practitioners who assert that hospices are unnecessary. Most would agree:

Like most general practitioners I believe that care of the dying is very much part of our job and we should look to the hospices to help us do this better—not to do it for us', (Akerman 1984).

In other words, when things are relatively straightforward, the primary care team will cope, and cope well. However, when the situation is more complex the need for additional help frequently becomes pressing.

In relation to good primary care the hospice has the following to offer (Charlton 1984):

1. The provision of a consultative advisory service.
2. The provision of specific treatment for symptoms, such as chronic obstructive lymphoedema.
3. Help with 'problem' patients, in respect of both physical symptoms and psychosocial needs.
4. Help with the young patient and those with young families.
5. Ongoing education concerning appropriate treatment for the terminally ill.

These are, however, obvious limits to co-operation. Hospices are sometimes accused of 'taking over' patient care and of excluding the general practitioner. If this happens, it is easy to understand a general practitioner's reluctance to refer a patient even when the situation is far from satisfactory. On the other hand, knowledge concerning pain and symptom control is still widely variable from area to area, and from general practitioner to general practitioner. Sometimes it is impossible for the hospice to do other than alter completely the general practitioner's therapeutic regimen. Almost certainly this will require taking over the therapeutic aspects of care for several weeks. Even here, though, as terminal care is more than therapeutics, there is no need for the general practitioner to feel totally excluded.

Those who work in a hospice agree with those in primary care that home for most patients is best, but this is not always possible. The proportion of home deaths varies in different parts of the country, from 2:1 at home (Woodbine 1982), through 1:1 home and hospital (Levy 1976; Keane et al. 1983), to 2:1 in hospital (Ford and Pincherle 1978; Reilly and Patten 1981). Although hospice care helps keep patients in the community (Annual Report 1983), a proportion will inevitably require admission when death is close. In such circumstances, 'Hospice is not a second best; it is an alternative best', (Thomson 1981).

CONCLUSION

Hospice care seeks to help patients and their family in a comprehensive manner. To be truly successful, it must be balanced:

Given the skill alone, however brilliant and sophisticated that skill may be, there can only be a clinical chill about the dying. Given friendship alone, however warm that friendship may be, there will be needless suffering and discomfort. Given both, you have the main ingredients which go to the helping of a man to die with dignity. Given a living faith, there can be added an element of triumph, for death is then viewed not as a terminus but as a junction.   (Coggan 1977)

REFERENCES

Akerman, F. (1984). Hospices. *British Medical Journal* **288**, 1996.
Annual Report (1983). Macmillan Continuing Care Team in the Camberwell Health Authority.
Buckingham, R. W., Lack, S. A., Mount, B. M., MacLean, L. D. and Collins, J. J. (1976). Living with the dying: use of the technique of participant observation. *Canadian Medical Association Journal* **115**, 1211–5.
Charlton, M. (1984). *Personal communication*.
Coggan, D. (1977). On dying and dying well. Moral and spiritual aspects. *Proceedings of the Royal Society of Medicine* **70**, 75–81.
Ford, G. R. and Pincherle, G. (1978). Arrangements for terminal care in the National Health Service (especially those for cancer patients). *Health Trends* **10**, 73–6.
Frankl, V. (1963). *Man's search for meaning*. Pocket Books, New York.
Greer, D. S., Mor, V., Sherwood, S., Morris, J. N. and Birnbaum, H. (1983). National hospice study analysis plan. *Journal of Chronic Diseases* **36**, 737–80.
Hardy, A. C. (1979). The spiritual nature of man. Clarendon Press, Oxford.
Hinton, J. (1979). Comparison of places and policies for terminal care. *Lancet* **i**, 29–32.
Kane, R. L., Wales, J., Bernstein, L., Leibowitz, A. and Kaplan, S. (1984). A randomized controlled trial of hospice care. *Lancet* **i**, 890–4.
Keane, W. G., Gould, J. H. and Millard, P. H. (1983). Death in practice. *Journal of the Royal College of General Practitioners* **33**, 347–51.
Kubler-Ross, E. (1970). *On death and dying*. Tavistock, London.
Lack, S. A. and Buckingham, R. W. (1978). *First American Hospice*. Hospice Inc. New Haven, Conn.
Levy, B. (1976). Fatal illness in general practice. *Journal of the Royal College of General Practitioners* **26**, 303–7.
Luxton, R. W. (1979). The modern hospice and its challenge to medicine. *British Medical Journal* **ii**, 583–4.
Melzack, R., Ofeisch, J. G. and Mount, B. M. (1976). The Brompton Mixture: effects on pain in cancer patients. *Canadian Medical Association Journal* **115**, 125–8.
Mount, B. M. (1976). Report of Pilot Project, Palliative Care Services, Royal Victorian Hospital, Montreal.
—— (1980). Hospice care. *Journal of the Royal Society of Medicine* **73**, 471–3.
—— and Scott, J. F. (1983). Whither hospice evaluation? *Journal of Chronic Diseases* **36**, 731–6.
National Hospice Organization (USA) (1981). Standards of a hospice program of care.
O'Donovan, O. (1982). *Some theological questions about death and dying*. Paper

given 1 February 1982 to Oxford Field Group of Institute of Religion and Medicine.

Parkes, C. M. (1972). Accuracy of predictions of survival in later stages of cancer. *British Medical Journal* **ii**, 29–31.

—— (1979*a*). Terminal care: evaluation of inpatient service at St. Christopher's Hospice. I. Views of surviving spouse on effects of the service on the patient. *Postgraduate Medical Journal* **55**, 517–22.

—— (1979*b*). Terminal care: evaluation of inpatient service at St. Christopher's Hospice. II. Self-assessment of effects of the service on surviving spouse. *Postgraduate Medical Journal* **55**, 523–7.

Reilly, P. M. and Pattern, M. P. (1981). Terminal care in the home. *Journal of the Royal College of General Practitioners* **31**, 531–7.

Smith, T. (1984). Problems of hospices. *British Medical Journal* **288**, 1178–9.

Stedeford, A. (1984). *Facing death: Patients, families and professionals.* Heinemann, London.

Thompson, I. (1984). Ethical issues in palliative care. In *Palliative care. The management of far-advanced illness.* (D. Doyle, ed.) pp. 461–85. Croom Helm, London and Canberra; Charles Press, Philadelphia.

Thomson, W. A. R. (1981). The hospice tradition. *Journal of the Royal Society of Medicine* **74**, 90–1.

Twycross, R. G. (1982). Euthanasia: a physician's viewpoint. *Journal of Medical Ethics* **8**, 86–95.

—— (1984). *A time to die.* Christian Medical Fellowship Publications, London.

Wilkes, E., Crowther, A. G. O. and Greaves, C. W. K. H. (1978). A different kind of day hospital—for patients with preterminal cancer and chronic disease. *British Medical Journal* **ii**, 1053–6.

Woodbine, G. (1982). The care of the patients dying from cancer. *Journal of the Royal College of General Practitioners* **32**, 685–9.

FURTHER READING

Doyle, D. (1984). *Palliative care. The management of far-advanced illness.* Croom Helm, London and Canberra: Charles Press, Philadelphia.

Saunders, C. M. (1984). *The management of terminal disease* (2nd edn). Edward Arnold, London.

7 The dying child: a hospice for children

Frances Dominica

INTRODUCTION

Helen House, Oxford, a hospice for children, opened in November 1982 to offer respite care and terminal care on a home-from-home basis to children with life-threatening disease. It is thought to be the first of its kind in the world.

Starting from the belief that home is almost always the best possible place for a child who cannot benefit further from attempts at curative therapy, Helen House aims to ease the strain for those families who care for their child at home by offering respite care at intervals, and to make it possible for other families to have their child at home, who, without the offer of respite care might find it necessary to leave the child in full-time residential care. The ideal shared by members of the Helen House team is to offer support and friendship to children who have life-threatening or profoundly handicapping disease, and to their families, trying to be sensitive in responding to their individual needs, and so enabling both child and family to achieve the optimum quality of life; to help the child to die with dignity if and when the time comes; and then to help the family to live on after the death of their child.

Helen House was not a carefully formulated hospice programme planned, as it were, in the abstract, but rather the actualization of an idea which grew out of the tragic illness of one small child. For this reason it is important to describe Helen's history at some length because each detail has bearing on the vision and ideals out of which Helen House has grown and now functions.

HELEN

In August 1978, a small child was admitted to an acute-care hospital in Oxford with a three-week history and signs of raised intracranial pressure. Helen was then two-and-a-half years old and previously had been a bright, happy child. Investigations showed evidence of a massive cerebral tumour which was surgically removed the day following admission. Postoperatively, Helen haemorraged and began convulsing.

The dying child

A chance encounter a few days after Helen's initial surgery led to a growing friendship with her family. As a trained nurse, it was a new experience for me to be deeply involved with a child during hospitalization, not this time in a professional capacity, but simply as a friend of the family. This afforded the opportunity of seeing things through their eyes, sharing their anxieties and their hopes, feeling both the gratitude and the frustration of being heavily dependent on professionals within the hospital for the well-being of Helen and for such information as they might choose to impart or to withhold concerning her condition and prognosis. One saw a gradual change between an all-out attempt to promote recovery, whether it be total or partial, to the reluctant acceptance that Helen's condition was not responding, and would not respond to treatment. It was hard for everyone concerned, professionals as well as parents, to adjust from an attitude of hope to one of knowing that she would never get well. There is always a danger of saying in a situation like this, whether with words or manner, 'There is nothing more we can do'.

A brain scan six months after surgery showed sufficiently conclusive results to convince Helen's parents that nothing useful could be achieved by prolonging her stay in hospital; it had become an inappropriate environment for her. With her neurosurgeon's full agreement, she was taken home where she has been cared for by her parents ever since. She was then just three years old and her sister had been born one month before Helen left hospital.

However competent and intelligent parents are, it can be a frightening and isolating experience to leave an acute-care hospital with the round-the-clock skill and support it offers and to find oneself alone at home with a gravely ill child. Even frequent home visits of doctors, nurses, and other members of the health team leave the parents on their own with the child for the major part of the 24 hours of every day and particularly through the long, lonely hours of the night. Helen suffered frequent convulsions and often seemed distressed but had no means of communicating the cause of her distress; she frequently had very disturbed nights. The physical strain of caring for her day and night, as well as caring for a new-born child, began to tell on her parents, but this was nothing by comparison with the exhaustion from the prolonged grief they were suffering. Very tentatively, I asked if they would trust me enough to 'lend' me Helen sometimes. Over the next three years, she came to our convent in Oxford on a number of occasions. We would put up her cot or a small bed in my room and I would look after her for a few days about six times a year. Because I knew the nursery rhymes she had loved before she was ill and which her parents continued to sing to her; because I knew that she had hated baked beans before she was ill and that they still taste of baked beans even if they are put through a liquidizer; because they believed that I loved her as a person with a spirit and with feelings as well as a body, they were content to entrust her to me. This enabled them to have the luxury of a few unbroken nights' sleep, the chance to concentrate on the other children (three and five years younger than Helen), or to take an occasional holiday. There was also the relief of knowing that if Helen's mother was herself unwell, there was somewhere that Helen was known and could be cared for.

During one of Helen's early visits the idea occurred of extending what had, by then, become a very special friendship with Helen and her parents to other gravely ill children and their families. We would not be offering a long-term facility but rather supporting families who wanted to care for their sick child at home. With encouragement and advice from many people concerned in the well-being of such children and their families, plans for Helen House were drawn up and a leaflet giving information and asking for financial help was distributed in 1980. Within a year the general public had given the necessary £500 000 to build, furnish, and equip the hospice and construction began, the site being in the grounds of the convent in Oxford. Building took one year to complete and during this year a further £500 000 towards an endowment fund for future running costs was given through voluntary sources. Helen House received its first young visitors in November 1982, just three years since the original concept of the idea, Helen, herself, being then almost seven years old.

THE BUILDING

Helen House is set in three acres of well-established and beautiful gardens. It is a minute's walk from shops and a bus route to the city centre which is one-and-a-half miles away. The house has accommodation for eight children at any one time and provision is made for parents and siblings to be also resident if they wish. Of the eight individually designed and furnished children's bedrooms, two pairs of two have inter-communicating double doors, making it possible to have two double rooms in place of four single rooms. Advantage is taken of this when two children of the same family visit, or if children make friends with each other and choose to share. It is interesting to note that most children consider their bedroom as their territory and seem to enjoy the security and the privacy it can provide. Six of the bedrooms have a window-seat which converts to a comfortable divan where a parent may choose to sleep, but most parents prefer the appartment designed for their use upstairs, with its two double bedrooms, sitting room, kitchen, and bathroom. The main playroom has glass doors opening out into the garden; a small hobbies room has easy-clean surfaces for messy activities and another playroom is used for

116 *The dying child*

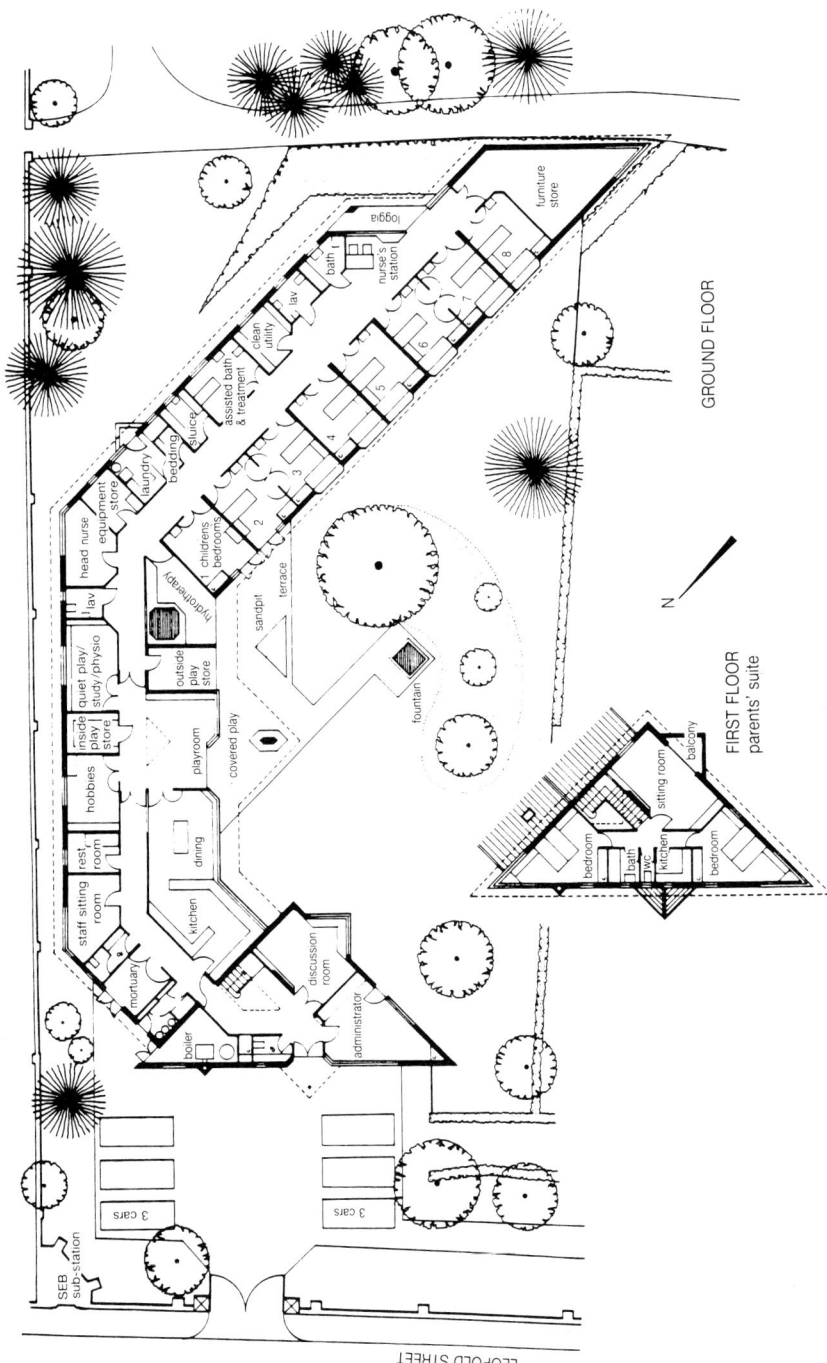

Fig. 7.1. The plans of Helen House, Oxford. (Reproduced by permission of Bicknell and Hamilton, Chartered Architects, 1 Charlotte Street, London W1P 1HD.)

reading and listening to tapes or as a dayroom for a child confined to bed. The jacuzzi, a gift from the Royal Air Force, is not only a pleasure to children who are mobile and alert, despite their disease, but is also of tremendous benefit to those suffering varying degrees of paralysis, immobility or emaciation and often evokes delighted response from children rarely known to respond to any kind of stimulus. The kitchen with dining area is designed in farmhouse-style is a natural focal point of the house, children, parents, and staff who eat together and often share in the preparation of meals and the washing of dishes! A room resembling an ordinary bedroom, but with a cooling system, is available for use when a child dies in Helen House and parents and relatives are able to spend time there with their child.

The staff of Helen House are all non-resident. This is a deliberate policy as it is felt to be important that they live away from what is inevitably emotionally taxing and often draining work.

Every possible emphasis has been laid upon making the house resemble home rather than hospital or institution, both in architectural design and in the choice of fabrics and furniture. The house is carpeted, each room has different curtain fabric, and much of the furniture, including the beds and cots, was designed and made in ash by a local craftsman. Machine-washable continental quilts with attractive covers are used for all children. Light, colour, and space were of prime important to the design team.

THE TEAM

The team caring for the families in Helen House consists of approximately 20 full-time (or equivalent) members of staff. These include registered nurses with specialist paediatric training, teachers, a nursery nurse, social worker, physiotherapist, a chaplain, and others, some of whom are parents themselves. There is minimal emphasis on hierarchy although there is a head nurse and deputy head nurse. No-one is employed specifically as cook or cleaner, each person shares these activities. The medical director is in general practice, based in the immediate vicinity and he visits the house regularly once a week, with frequent shorter visits during the week, and otherwise by request. With only a small number of our children suffering from malignant disease and requiring pain relief and symptom control, part-time medical input is sufficient. Members of staff do not wear a uniform and are known by their first names. In selecting the team, it was recognized that it was essential to have people with the right qualifications and experience, but the greatest emphasis was laid upon their personal qualities and on whether they 'spoke the same language'. The final selection relied heavily upon the intuition of the selectors.

LIAISON WITH OTHER AGENCIES AND WITH FAMILIES

One member of staff, a trained social worker, is employed to work part-time in the house on the ordinary duty rota and part-time in the community, visiting children and their families at home or in hospital, and liaising with other agencies involved in caring for the families. Where, for example, a family doctor, home tutor or physiotherapist who cares for the child when he is at home is willing to continue to be involved on a practical level during the child's visits to Helen House, they are encouraged to do so, continuity being seen as vitally important for both child and family. However, distance and other practical difficulties often make this impossible.

Specialists in many fields of medicine offer their services free of charge on a consultancy basis and, although Helen House is an independent facility, it works closely with National Health Service (NHS) where this is appropriate.

Home care

A home care service has not yet been developed on a formal basis and at present Helen House works in liaison with the existing domiciliary paediatric nurses employed by the NHS. Where distance permits, members of the team do give help and support in the child's own home when the need arises, but this is on an informal basis.

Staff support

A consultant child psychiatrist acts as a facilitator at a weekly staff support group, offering an opportunity for open discussion among members of the team about matters of mutual concern. There is also the opportunity to share some of the joys and sorrows, perplexities, and misunderstandings which inevitably occur. Everyone recognizes that despite the genuinely happy and informal atmosphere which prevails in the House, it is inevitably linked with grief in its many forms and considerable emotional demands are made on the staff day-by-day. An essential attribute for members of the team is a sense of humour! It is vital to care for the carers.

Administration and finance

An administrator and a secretary manage the administration of Helen House. The annual running costs amount to approximately £180 000, all of which comes from voluntary sources. The House does not employ anyone as fund-raiser but nationwide support and interest continues to grow. No charge is made to families using Helen House, either for the children or their relatives, as it is felt that many of them have already suffered considerable financial strain through the sickness of their child.

'HOSPICE' AND 'TERMINAL ILLNESS'

It seems important to define the word 'hospice' at this point. The Oxford English Dictionary definition is: 'a house of rest and entertainment for pilgrims, travellers or strangers—for the destitute or sick'. A petition to Henry VIII in 1538 reads: 'For the ayde and comforte of the poor sykke, blynde, aged and impotent personnes ... whereyn they may be lodged, cherysshed and refreshed' (Clay 1966). Hospices have been in existence in one form or another since about AD 475 and were particularly in evidence in the Middle Ages during which time they were places where pilgrims and travellers could receive refuge and sustenance. The religious orders who were responsible for the hospices started caring for the sick and dying, and gradually the term 'hospice' came to be associated increasingly with this aspect of the work. During the nineteenth century the charitable hospitals in England started to refuse admitting incurables and workhouse infirmaries catered solely for the destitute. Hospices, therefore, came to provide an alternative to either of these. Latterly, hospices have been associated mainly with the care of the terminally ill. One of the forerunners in the specialist care of the dying was St. Joseph's Hospice in East London and it was here in the 1950s that Dame Cicely Saunders began to develop her methods of pain control in the terminally ill and chronic sick and to pioneer the modern hospice movement. In 1967, under her leadership, St. Christopher's Hospice was opened. Here, as in some other hospice units, it is deliberate policy to care not only for those in the last weeks or months of life but also to offer respite (or in some cases long-term) care to those with chronic illness.

Despite the efforts of many working within the hospice movement, the popular idea amongst the vast majority of the general public is that all hospices cater exclusively for the dying. However, continuing care units, if the term were not so cumbersome, might be the more appropriate term.

Six months before Helen House opened, a father asked if we could help to care for his three-year-old son who was 'terminally ill'. Explaining that as Helen House was not yet open and that very regretfully we could not help, the father replied that this was all right; he was in any case thinking in terms of the time when the hospice would be open. 'My son has been terminally ill for two years', he said. At one year of age the little boy had been diagnosed as having a life-threatening condition with a prognosis of not more than five years, and from the time his parents understandably described him as terminally ill.

THE SELECTION OF CHILDREN

Priority is given to children in the final stage of illness. In the West, statistics show that a high percentage of children who die, do so in hospital. In cases of acute infection or accident this is clearly the right place, with all the facilities for saving life where this is possible and appropriate. However, in other situations it is very often the wish of the family to have their child die at home and, given the right kind of support, this is both possible and desirable. On the other hand, it is important that we do not generalize when assessing the best course of action for any individual family as each one has different reactions and needs. No family should be coerced into having their child at home to die against their wishes or made to feel that they are 'bad' parents if they decide not to. Sometimes parents feel they could not bear to continue to live in the house where their child has died and would have to move house if the child died at home. Others may have seen other people's children, with the same disease as their child, dying by haemorrage or in convulsion or with pain, and may prefer to be in an environment where they feel totally supported and surrounded by people who will know how to meet all eventualities. Sometimes, the child himself will feel more secure in a place where he knows there are doctors and nurses. We have known each of these situations exist, even when home care support has been available, and the feelings of child and family must be respected.

When a child, who is in the final stage of illness comes to Helen House, any members of the immediate family are also welcomed and encouraged to stay with us and to be with their child and care for him as much as they feel willing and able to do so.

Babies in the first weeks of life are sometimes referred to us from special care baby units of hospitals. If it is recognized that a baby has a condition which is not compatible with life, and curative therapy is either not attempted or is abandoned at an early stage, it is conceivable that an intensive care unit ceases to be the appropriate environment for the infant and his parents. The parents may not feel sufficiently confident to take their baby home and the solution can sometimes be a half-way house such as Helen House is able to provide.

Children in the final stage of illness, however, form a minority of those who come to Helen House, the majority being in varying stages of chronic, life-threatening disease, for example, cystic fibrosis, muscular dystrophy, biliary atresia, pulmonary atresia, Batten's disease, Trisomy 18, and the mucopolysaccharide diseases—Sanfillipo, Hurler's disease, Hunter's disease, etc. Children who come suffering with malignant disease most often come towards the end of their life and therefore come into the category mentioned above, but a common exception to this are children with cerebral tumours where curative therapy has been abandoned but where the disease then spans a considerable length of time.

A third and necessarily very small category consists of children with profound handicap whose condition appears to change little, if at all, but whose handicap is so severe that it is in itself a threat to life. These children frequently live on with an uneventful history and then die suddenly of respiratory infection, kidney failure, major convulsion, sometimes with the onset of puberty. One of the biggest problems is the selection of children in this category, to try to take into account not only the severity of the child's condition but also the needs of the family as a whole. It is always distressing to have to refuse requests from families whose children suffer from cerebral palsy, for example, but we recognize that the demand would be greater than could be met and it is felt preferable not to make an initial commitment to a family which, in all probability, cannot be fulfilled.

Many of the children who come to Helen House has diseases which cause brain damage and mental retardation along with other effects. Others, however, are mentally alert and active, although restricted in their physical activity. In planning the children's visits we try to arrange for mentally alert children to have the companionship of others equally alert so that they can provide stimulation for each other. Loneliness, boredom, and frustration, through not being able to join in with the activities of their siblings and peers, are often among these children's greatest problems and they look to Helen House, when they visit, for stimulation, entertainment, and company: 'I am bored at home and I've fallen out with my parents. Would you book me into the Snoopy room for next week, please?'

Parents and siblings of all children are welcome to stay for part or all of their child's visits. This is particularly encouraged on the initial visit so that the family can teach us how best to care for their child, especially if he is unable to communicate himself; for without doubt, they are the people who know their child best and we have much to learn from them. It also gives us the opportunity of getting to know the family, and the family the opportunity of getting to know us, in the hope of establishing a relationship of friendship and trust.

Irrespective of race or belief, children who can benefit from our type of hospice care are welcomed; the ages range from birth to 18 years, and our catchment areas covers the United Kingdom.

PATTERN OF VISITS

Children coming for respite care either come at regular intervals (for example, two weeks in every two months, one week in every six weeks, alternative weekends), or by arrangement with the family. Some ask only for occasional help in order to cover a holiday or a period of crisis at home. A child would not normally come for more than a month on any one visit unless the circumstances are exceptional as long-term institutional care is not provided. It is important for the child to believe that he belongs at home with his family and just comes to visit Helen House from time to time, as he might visit friends.

REFERRALS

Initial enquiries come from many sources including the family, doctors, nurses, social workers and others in the health team, and sometimes from teachers. All we require when we have decided that there is a family to whom we can offer help is that the parents wish to accept our offer and that the doctor responsible for the child's care is in agreement, and is willing to pass on details of the illness and treatment.

CASE HISTORIES

The spirit of Helen House and its objectives are best illustrated by the case histories of several of its young visitors.

Michael

Michael was diagnosed at birth as having cystic fibrosis. This was a devastating blow to his parents, both nearly 40 when he was born. They already had six daughters and Michael was their longed-for son. The family was poor, socially deprived, and lived in a rough district on the outskirts of a large sprawling city.

When the family was first referred to us Michael was 12 years old and the disease was far advanced. His mother could see no future for her son, whilst his father, unable to articulate his feelings, simply could not accept the inevitable outcome. Helen House was so totally different from their own home environment that the parents reacted in a predictable way on their first visit—they surrounded Michael with fierce protectiveness and made his room a safe fortress for themselves. With our agreement his drugs were kept in his room and administered by his parents, as was his physiotherapy.

It took several stays at Helen House before the family began to relax, Gradually they learned to trust the staff and allow us more contact with their son. The mother began to talk freely and at length about her feelings, depression, the trials and tribulations of her life, and family. They began to enjoy their visits and where encouraged to go on various trips and excursions, usually organized by the staff. Always, though, their overriding concern was Michael and their determination to do everything for him themselves was understood and accepted.

More and more they began to lean on the staff for support and comfort in their grief over Michael's deteriorating condition. The father, although by this time, more comfortable and relaxed in Helen House, suffered silently from his helplessness to alter the inexorable progress of the disease and found his only relief in constantly entertaining his son, buying him expensive toys and games and bringing him whatever he thought would please him. The mother's grief was more overt, expressing itself in bouts of depression; during one visit she was taken to the local hospital suffering from angina and heart failure, aggravated by gross obesity.

We began to recognize our role with this family. Family togetherness was everything to them. Fiercely loyal and bonded together, in spite of the enormous problems of each individual member of the family, they still needed us and turned to us constantly for support, strength, and friendship. Initially, the mother had vehemently denied that Michael had any conception of the true nature of his illness but, as the months went by, she felt able to accept the truth that Michael was well aware of the implications and she passed over to us the task that was too painful for her—that of answering Michael's questions honestly. Finally, she herself was able to tolerate his remarks about death although she could never actually bring herself to admit the certainty of it to him.

When Michael was in the terminal stages of his illness the parents telephoned in great anguish feeling they could no longer cope despite the excellent support of their social worker and general practitioner. They came to Helen House and Michael, now bed-ridden, always had at least one of them with him. His mother slept in his room, older sisters travelled down frequently to be with him, and his room became their home where they clung together for support. They were now quite comfortable with us and reached out to us for warmth and our support. Finally the father's reserve broke and he was able to weep.

As the days passed and Michael became weaker, the father became greatly agitated; he had an overwhelming desire to take his son back to where he belonged—home. He felt it was not right to deprive Michael's sisters of these last days, and after initial opposition, the mother came to be in full agreement. Immediately we arranged an ambulance and staff escort. The father went on ahead and when we arrived at home it was moving to see the whole family waiting at the door to receive their brother home. They had prepared his room with tender care and surrounded him with their love. He died 10 days later.

With this family our work was not so much with the child (with whom we were allowed only miminal contact), but with the parents, enabling them, perhaps, to get through the last painful year of Michael's life, and providing the moral support and friendship which helped them to find the strength and confidence to care for him in their own home at the end.

Joseph

Joseph was born with Fanconi's anaemia, diagnosed at the age of two-and-a-half. He was treated with anabolic steroids which unfortunately caused hepatic tumours by the time he was six years old. He was therefore given alternative treatment of five-weekly transfusions of blood and platelets.

The mother and father were intelligent, with a very strong religious faith. There were two other children, a boy of five and a girl of nine, and in 1984 they had another baby girl. They are very closely knit family—they have, in fact, only used Helen House on four occasions.

Joseph made a deep impression on all who met him; a very intelligent boy of 11, he was immensely articulate and his philosophy of life and death provided much food for thought. He was also a normal, mischievious boy with a great sense of humour. His condition was worsening and his suffering considerable. The parents, like so many parents, suffered prolonged anticipatory grieving; time and again they were told, on sound medical evidence, that Joseph's death was imminent and yet, against all the odds, Joseph lived on.

Because the family visited so rarely, an occasional home visit was made at their request and it quickly became evident that they wished these visits to be regular and frequent. They seemed to consider them of the utmost importance. As the friendship with the family deepened these outwardly coping parents were able to reveal their intense inner sufferings, desperation, and overwhelming grief. Being articulate, they were able to explain that it was not often necessary actually to come to Helen House but it was of extreme importance to them to know that Helen House was there. Just knowing that they could come at any time they felt the need enabled them to keep going. The mother said that she looked upon Helen House as 'a maiden aunt'—always available and willing to help when needed! Their need, they said, was to feel the warmth and love and friendship coming to them from the hospice. They are extremely home-loving and it is quite traumatic for both Joseph and parents alike to leave the safety of their home and stay in another house. Perhaps the endless trips to hospital have contributed to this need to stay in the warmth and safety of their own home.

On one occasions, at the mother's request, she, the baby, and Joseph were fetched by Helen House staff and brought to the hospice for a day, which in the event, extended to an overnight stay. The visit seemed to clarify certain things for both mother and son. A baby was dying in the hospice at the time and Joseph's mother asked many searching questions about how we were going to cope with the parents' grief, how soon the child would be taken from them to the mortuary, etc. She was shown our little 'rest-room' and assured that the baby would not be taken away until the parents felt ready. It was clear that Joseph's mother was actually relating the events to her own forthcoming experience.

When the baby eventually died both Joseph and his mother went in to see him; Joseph, walking apprehensively towards the room where the dead child lay, experienced great relief and allayment of his own private fears.

Helping the family within their own home has also meant that the parents have been able to trust us enought to go out for an evening leaving the children in our care. They have also allowed us to stay, on two occasions, with Joseph in the hospital during his traumatic blood transfusions.

We are learning that hospice work can be infinitely flexible, accommodating the great variety of needs expressed by our families, each one unique.

Sammy

Sammy was diagnosed at the age of four as having a stage IV non-Hodgkin's Lymphoma involving the ileum with secondary deposits in the bone marrow. At the time of diagnosis he had a six-week history of intermittent abdominal pain with severe occurrences 10–20 times a day, associated with vomiting 1–5 times a day. He underwent a course of chemotherapy, but in view of the high likelihood of disease relapse on standard chemotherapy, it was felt that the only possibility of long-term survival would be with bone marrow transplanation following total body irradiation. However, it proved impossible to find a perfect match and he therefore underwent an autologous bone marrow graft.

Initially he did well, apart from two brief episodes of right facial palsy, but one month later he complained of headache, vomiting, and lethargy, and lumbar puncture revealed numerous blasts. It was concluded that there had been a focal deposit of lymphomatous cells which resisted radiation treatment and rapidly recurred. Sammy's young parents were fully involved in discussion about his prognosis and future management. His central nervous system relapse during the period of marrow regeneration was only partially controlled with intrathecal chemotherapy and a course of palliative cranial irradiation. Acute-care hospital ceased to be the appropaite environment and it was suggested that the family might like to visit Helen House to see if it was a place they would choose to come to if the situation became unmanageable at home. Sammy, his parents, and three-year-old sister, spend a day with us. Sammy had kept asking if they could have a holiday, but his parents had never been able to afford this. When he saw Helen House for the first time he exclaimed: 'It's a real holiday camp! Can we stay here?' and cried miserably when his parents told him they could not stay here this time. His condition deteriorated rapidly over the next few days and the whole family returned to us for the last five days of his life.

Pain control was one of the most urgent problems and this was achieved fairly satisfactorily after a day or two. Sammy improved a little and was able to enjoy playing and being taken out in a pushchair. There were many moments of real pleasure interspersed with the times when he clearly felt very ill indeed. His parents took it in turns to be with him day and night. He developed minor nose bleeds and haematuria and was given platelets to prevent fatal haemorrage—the form of death witnessed by his parents in another child and which they dreaded more than anything. Sammy died suddenly and peacefully the following morning, having been fully conscious to the end.

His grandparents came the next day to see him for the last time, to be with his grief-stricken parents and little sister and to see the room and 'holiday camp' that they knew Sammy had loved. At the end of the day, they took the little girl home with them and Sammy's parents asked if they could stay with us during the three days until the funeral. Sometimes alone together and sometimes with us, talking of Sammy before he was ill, of his illness, of the future without him, crying with us, sharing meals with us, and sitting up with us late into the night, they now talk of those days as a time when the healing began. Two of us went with them to their home town on the South Coast for Sammy's funeral. We knew that returning home was hard for them.

We keep in touch with the family with fairly frequent telephone calls, and they, like all our other bereaved families, accepted our invitation to visit us and plan to spend part of their summer holiday in Helen House.

THE CHILD AND HIS FAMILY

The physical care of a child who has a life-threatening disease is only a small part of the care he needs. His emotional and spiritual needs and those of his family are of equal importance. Caring for such a child is about caring for the whole child and his family, helping them to achieve the optimum quality of life throughout, even though the life span may be short, enabling the child to meet diminishment of health or death with dignity and helping the family to live on. We must be sensitive to the very different needs of each person and be ready to respond in the way which it is most appropriate to each individual.

Although families in previous generations faced the same kind of tragedy much more often, the existence of the close-knit extended family and the greater involvment of the local community provided the kind of support which is lacking today. Today's nuclear family, not infrequently a single-parent family, can suffer terrible feelings of loneliness and isolation. One of our tasks in a children's hospice is to try to supply some of the missing elements by offering active friendship on a regular and reliable basis, often extending over many years.

Our children are a part of the family to which they belong and they cannot be seen other than in that context. Some of our families face immense practical problems, but these are seldom the worst of the difficulties. However imaginative and understanding we may be, we can only begin to be aware of the strain and anguish which the family experiences physically and emotionally. With an acute illness or accident followed by death, the grieving process and mourning have the potential of being resolved over a period of time. Objectively, at least, others accept this process. With chronic sickness the grief is terribly prolonged and may often begin from the moment of diagnosis where it is recognized that there is no known cure, and there is not the same possibility of resolving or completing the mourning. Every stage of diminished ability or independence, every loss of function, and each new sign of deterioration is a further cause of mourning to the family and needs the acknowledgement of those involved, not least those professionally concerned.

We need to recognize that father and mother may react in very different ways to their distress and the relationship may become strained because of the difficulty of one partner in understanding how or why the other is behaving in a certain way. Sheer physical exhaustion may affect communication and so things go from bad to worse. One or both partners may feel ashamed or guilty about their child's disorder and their own inadequacy in coping with it. It is generally easier and more acceptable for a woman to show her emotions than it is for a man and it is particularly difficult for him in the social or work context. It is also traditional for her to fulfil the nurturing, caring role which reinforces the bond between mother and child, sometimes to the apparent exclusion of the father. Either parent may have periods of time when they distance themselves from the child as a form of self-protection. Arguments occur about the treatment and management of the child. It is not for us to take sides, but rather to be sensitive to the difficulties which each faces and to make positive suggestions about activities they and their child may be able to enjoy together.

There is a temptation for relatives to over-indulge a child by showering him with material gifts or allowing antisocial behaviour, and we have to try to help them to see that this often adds to the child's feeling of bewilderment. He needs a recognized structure for his own security in this world of his where many things have deviated from the norm. His need is for physical and emotional love and strength, rather than material possessions. The disruption of family life inevitably affects other children in the family who may feel neglected in favour of the sick child, and in some cases this can lead to strong resentment, resulting in disturbed behaviour. Their sorrow may manifest itself in many ways and not always be recognized. A sibling may have fears that he himself may suffer the same illness or even die and he may well feel that he must protect his already overburdened parents from this and other anxieties or strong emotions. Siblings who suffer from the same condition, for example, inherited progressive disorders, as some of our children do, have their own very special needs. We try to be here as friend and confidante to the siblings, and explanation and involvement appropriate to the age and temperament of the child may help to overcome some of the difficulties.

Grandparents and other relatives, as well as friends and neighbours, are affected by the child's suffering and we have to be aware that as well as being a potential source of help they can be potential casualties in the unfolding of a particular tragedy. Brothers and sisters need to be encouraged to enjoy their own friendships and not to feel guilty about this.

As we come to know members of a family well, it is sometimes possible for us to help them to encourage their sick child to enjoy such independence as he can, even though it may be minimal, rather than cling to what is so often the instinctive approach—to protect at all costs. Gradually, we try to build up a relationship of mutual trust and acceptance with the child by behaving consistently and invariably responding honestly. Sometimes a child trusts us enough to be able to relax and share some of his worst anxieties.

Mum and Dad think I don't know, but I have got cystic fibrosis, and when you've got that, you don't live long. I'll probably be dead in a year or two. What do you think it is like when you are dead?

I am frightened, 'cos if I die my Mummy can't come with me.

What will my parents do when I die? I *mustn't* die.

It is vital to listen carefully to what the child is actually saying or asking—adults easily fall into the trap of assuming that he is asking a more complex question than he really is. Our cardinal rule is never to lie to a child. This does not mean to say that he must be given the whole stark truth in one blow, but one is often able to give truthful reassurance and allay the child's fears about the actual process of dying and death itself, always, of course, using terms which the child understands and being careful not to contradict beliefs held by his family.

We find that the small child has a natural capacity for being able to live for the present moment and recognizing this can be used to advantage by those caring for him. If he is free of pain and discomfort and is surrounded by people he loves and trusts, he is less likely to be fearful for the future. The older child will have taken on more of the fears and complexities of an adult in facing dying and death. It must be categorically stated that there are no hard and fast ways of answering his questions or set methods of helping him come to terms with the truth. So much depends on our own ability to absorb the impact of the emotional and spiritual implications and cope with them ourselves. Platitudes and pat answers are less than helpful. At times when there seems to be nothing to say, it is better not to use empty words but rather try to communicate reassurance through physical presence—just being there through it all. We often remark how protective sick children feel towards their parents and to what great lengths they will go to spare them further pain, whereas someone they trust who is less closely related, but has some authority, may be taken into the child's confidence.

The family may well feel inadequate in caring for the child as his condition deteriorates and they need constant reassurance and encouragement to be involved on every level as far as they are able. They often have fears and fantasies, as to the mode of dying and, if these can be expelled, a little of the anguish may be removed. Through all the strain of caring for a chronically sick child, there will almost inevitably have been moments when parents have wished it would all end. When the end of the child's life is actually in sight, this may result in great feelings of guilt. With the actual death of the child, the family needs to be helped through the appalling confusion of a mixture of relief and grief.

If the relationship has been one of trust and friendship, it will follow that it does not end with the death of the child. Bereavement, particulary when it centres around a child, is often a very lonely time. Friends and even relatives may find it an impossibly difficult task to be faced with the family's grief in all its varying forms of expression. They may be afraid of their own emotional reactions and the instinctive response is to stay away, hoping that the family will find support from others. Behaviour and remarks indicating that it is time the family 'got back to normal' can be devastatingly hurtful. We must remember that a family never gets over the death of their child, even though, in time, they may adjust. Their greatest need is to have a friend or friends who are prepared to stay alongside them, not only through the tears, but through the anger and accusations, the guilt and denial and all the bleak, inexpressible grief.

It is sometimes hard for us to understand why anger can be directed against those who have genuinely tried to offer help and friendship. We realize as time goes on that in situations where we do not honestly feel the anger or accusations are justified, we may have a role to play as scapegoat.

PRACTICAL CARE OF THE CHILD

Caring for children with life-threatening disease needs a great degree of flexibility and creative use of imagination. The child may well contribute some of the best ideas himself and it is important to consider these, even though he may issue commands and instructions in a demanding and cheeky manner. Necessary changes in treatment sometimes bring parents face-to-face with the harsh fact of further deterioration in their child's illness and we have to be sensitive and understanding in meeting their response and gaining their co-operation.

Meticulous attention must be given to the basic physical needs of the sick child, so avoiding or relieving discomfort or distress wherever possible—attention to skin, hair, mouth, diet, and bowel function, as well as the more specific pain relief and symptom control. Our children sometimes enjoy cooking or helping to choose and prepare a meal and shopping expeditions in the neighbourhood help to make it feel more like home. Attractive, easy-to-wear clothes, will boost the child's morale as well as those around him.

CONCLUSION

It is an immeasurable privilege and a humbling experience to be allowed to share in the care of a very sick child. We are alongside members of his family at a time when they are at their most vulnerable. We are there not just as professional care-givers but as fellow human beings who must be able to be trusted implicitly and with whom there need be no pretence. There are often times when we have nothing wise to say and when all we can do is stand by, not trying to set ourselves up as having the answers; simply by sharing in the pain, we may help to dissipate it a little.

Helen House is an attempt to offer an ordinary kind of friendship to people facing an extraordinary kind of grief. It is the friendship with one little girl and her family extended to other gravely ill children and their families.

FURTHER READING

Byrne, S. R., Mother Frances Dominica. and Baum, J. D. (1984). Helen House—a hospice for children: an analysis of the first year. *British Medical Journal* **289**, 1665–8.

Burne, S. R. (1982*a*). Hospice care for children. *British Medical Journal* **284**, 1400.

—— (1982*b*). Helen House—a hospice for children. *Health Visitor* **55**, 544–5.

—— (1984). A hospice for children in England. *Paediatrics 1984.* 73

Farrow, G. (1982). The soothing touch. *World Medicine* August, 39–42.

Mother Frances Dominica (1982). Helen House—a hospice for children. *Maternal and Child Health* **7**, 355–9.
—— (1984). The nursing care of the chronically sick or handicapped child. In: *The Physically Handicapped Child—An interdisciplinary approach*. (Gillian McCarthy, ed.). Faber, London.

REFERENCE

Clay, M. R. (1966). In: *The Medieval Hospital of England*. Barnes & Noble, New York.

8 Care of the family in dying and grieving: a pastoral approach

David Atkinson

INTRODUCTION

Given the low rate of church attendance in Britain, it is perhaps surprising that a very high proportion of those who die (95 per cent according to Argyle and Beit-Hallahmi 1975) have a religious funeral. This is, of course, partly due to the fact that when there is a death in the family, each parishioner has the right to ask the parish priest to officiate. Also, it is partly due to the long-established custom in this country of associating ritual mourning with a religious service. Thus for many who never attend church, it is still thought appropriate for a priest to conduct proceedings at the cemetery or the crematorium. However, there is more to it than merely establishment or custom. In a British survey conducted in 1970 by the Independent Television Authority, it was found that the word 'death' made 64 per cent of respondents think about 'God'. It also indicated that a much higher proportion of people (44 per cent) said they would talk to a clergyman if they were afraid of death, than said they would talk to their doctor (8 per cent). The sense of loss associated with death brings with it a host of questions which at their root are primarily religious: questions about life's meaning, about the value of relationships, about the pain of guilt and the need for forgiveness, about feeling 'at home' in the universe or feeling 'abandoned', about the search for markers and bearings at a time of loneliness. These existential questions surrounding the experience of death and grief have an inescapably religious dimension. Indeed, in their discussion of the survey figures quoted above Argyle and Beit-Hallahmi (1975) comment: 'It looks as if in Britain today, religion is seen by many people primarily as a means of dealing with death'. Certainly there is frequently an increase in religious attidues and feelings as people get older. Several studies have shown this to be true, despite the fact that ritualistic religious behaviour outside the home (like church attendance) diminishes with increasing age (Moberg 1973).

The clergyman who has had pastoral contact with a family over many months or years will usually be one of the first to be called when there is a death in the family. Even for those who have no formal religious allegiance, and who do not meet the clergyman until they see him at the crematorium door, it is still widely believed that there is something appropriate about the minister being 'involved' at the time of death. Somehow it is 'part of his job'.

The task in this chapter is to outline some of the features of this 'part of his job'. What are the tasks of pastoral care? What function does the pastor fulfil in his care of the family in dying and grieving? This chpater, will primarily be concerned with those whose death is to some extent expected, rather than with those whose death is sudden or accidental. It will also be limited to the perspectives of Christian pastoral care, while acknowledging that many other religious traditions have equivalent pastoral functions associated with dying and grieving.

WHAT IS PASTORAL CARE?

Many of the functions which traditionally used to be associated with the pastoral ministry—teaching or counselling, to give two examples—are now often associated more with other professions. Is there still a distinctive *pastoral* task for which the clergyman is peculiarly equipped? Is there indeed a profession of pastoral care which needs to some extent to be 'rediscovered'. I believe that there is.

It is the pastor's privilege to share with a family in their growth, their joys, and their times of health, as well as in the darker days of sickness and distress. The pastor's relationship with his congregation is not episodic, not called into life only at times of crisis. The pastor stands for a longer, more continuous relationship with a person than is true for almost any other professional 'helper'. It can and should be a relationship of trust and confidence. The pastor can become a companion to others on their life-journey, sharing with them his own experiences of personal need and of divine grace.

Alastair Campbell (1981, p. 15) well summarizes this aspect of the pastoral vision:

It is out of the consistency and depth of the caring person's own character that help is given to another. Because he has known within himself the sense of failure and lostness which the other feels, the steadfastness of wholeness he offers is grounded in human reality. The carer and the cared for are not on two sides of a divide which must be bridged by some form of expertise on the part of the one who cares. Pastoral care is grounded in mutuality, not in expertise; it is possible because we share a common humanity with all the splendour and all the fallibility which that implies. If *I* can find some courage, hope and transcendence in the midst of life, then I can help my fellow men find that same wholeness; for I know that I am no better than they, no wiser, no more deserving of such fulfilment ...

Such pastoral caring is by no means, of course, the sole prerogative of the 'professional'. With the renewed emphasis on 'every member ministry' and 'lay pastors' in some parts of the Christian Church, there is a growing rediscovery of the personal and pastoral benefits of belonging to a 'community of care'. Within the Christian Church, however, there are those who are called to a professional pastoral vocation. However, to be a 'professional' does not diminish the fact that this vocation is first and foremost the provision of a caring relationship. While it is right, indeed essential, for the professional pastor to acknowledge the importance of insights from the human sciences, interaction with other caring professions, the development of listening, and counselling skills, and so on, his primary gift to his congregation and to others is of himself in relationship with them.

Within such a relationship, the pastoral task at times becomes one of offering support, comfort, and meaning to people at times of change and crisis. Nowhere is this more important, or more difficult, than in the care of the dying and grieving. From his religious perspective, the pastor can bring an understanding that the deep existential concerns referred to above are real 'in their own right' and are not merely symptoms of something else. He brings into the pastoral relationship the awareness (whether he uses religious language or not) that these concerns are related to the reality of God, and to the nature of human life made in God's image.

The clergyman, along with the doctor and the funeral director, is one of the few who are permitted to break through the taboos associated with death. In the care of the dying and the bereaved, he has a very particular role, three aspects of which we will now examine in more detail.

First, the pastor is a *representative* figure, who publicly acknowledges the religious aspects of life, and whose personal presence in the face of death 'gives permission' for those in need to share their religious concerns and talk seriously (sometimes angrily) about them. He represents also the community of faith, and can in the name of the church as a caring community, take the initiative towards people in their times of family crisis. The pastor can serve as a bridge for people back into contact with their wider community, and at a time of bereavement this can facilitate the processes of readjustment and resolution.

Secondly, the pastor can be a *reconciling* figure. He can be available to make time to be with the dying patient and with the mourning family. If appropriate, he can minister the resources of grace which can bring emotional as well as spiritual sustenance. He can make available ways of handling guilt through forgiveness. He can show how faith is one of God's gifts to help us cope with uncertainty and change. The pastor's personal (if sometimes silent) presence can provide support and guidance while processes of reconciliation are undertaken towards God or towards others, or while the complicated emotions of loss are being worked through.

Thirdly, in the face of death, the pastor serves a *ritual* function. This can be seen, for example, in sacramental ministry to the sick or dying, and also at the funeral service which can be a most important event in aiding the processes of 'letting go' and in the work of grieving.

The pastor is thus concerned with the whole person in his or her inner life as well as with the person's relationships with others and with God. To some degree the clergyman can exercise these three functions for any who turn to him for help. This is, especially true towards his congregation with whom he has the privilege of a trust relationship. A trusted pastor has a unique role among other helpers in assisting the dying person come to terms with his death, and to 'die well', and in helping the grieving family to learn how to cope.

A THEOLOGICAL APPROACH TO DYING AND GRIEVING

Before examining pastoral care in more practical detail, it is important to indicate some of the theological groundwork on which such care depends. What has been lost to many of us is an adequate *interpretation* of death. The Christian pastor is bearer of a shared tradition of interpretation, and in his preaching as well as his pastoral care, he offers a theological understanding of the reality of death. We all need a framework of interpretation within which dying and grieving can be faced. Death shatters our settled world, whether it is a world of belief or of unbelief. Christian faith affirms that God offers us grace sufficient to help us to cope, and the Christian pastor is a minister of that grace.

Other religious traditions offer different interpretative frameworks; this chapter concentrates on one particular approach.

Earlier generations of Christian people made much more of 'preparing for a good death' than many would consider polite today. To give one example, the Book of Common Prayer of the Church of England (1662) includes this rubric for 'The Visitation of the Sick':

> Then shall the Minister examine whether he repent him truly of his sins, and be in charity with all the world; exhorting him to forgive, from the bottom of his heart, all persons who have offended him; and if he hath offended any other, to ask them forgiveness; and where he hath done injury or wrong to any man, that he make ammends to the uttermost of his power. And if he hath not before disposed of his goods, let him then be admonished to make his Will, and to declare his debts, what he oweth and what is owing to him; for the better discharging of his conscience, and the quietness of his Executors. But men should often be put in remembrance to take order for the setting of their temporal estates whilst they are in health.

The two themes underlying this rubric are clear: the *reality* of death must be taken seriously, and people should be helped to *prepare* for it. Too often, until very recently, and then only in certain contexts, death has been avoided in conversation. Referring to the denial of death by the bereaved person, and the reinforcement of that denial by many around the bereaved, Lily Pincus (1976) writes of a 'general conspiracy that death has not occurred'. Out of their own fear of death, or in order to avoid hurting the feelings of a dying relative, families have sometimes failed to give honest support while, in fact, their loved one dies alone. The too ready modern assumption that death should take place in hospital has underlined this unwillingness to face reality. If the dying can be institutionalized, then its demand, and the need for care to be offered by the family, can be minimized. Together with this tendency to avoid facing death's reality, goes an unreadiness adequately to prepare for death. As the Prayer Book rubric indicated, a person can die with less stress if his personal relationships are healthy, his temporal affairs in order, and his conscience clear.

Christian theology offers an interpretation of death which seeks to account for the fact that in one sense it is the most natural, and yet in another sense the most unnatural of events. We all have to face the moment when, as Karl Barth (1935) puts it, 'The time we shall then have will be a time with a present (and with our whole past behind us), but with no future ... though we still are, we shall be no longer'. Death faces us with the edge of our existence. Because our time is finite, our time is therefore, whether we are conscious of it or not, overshadowed by death. What meaning can be given, then, to the fact that our existence in time—our 'natural life'—comes so unnaturally to an end? As Ernest Becker (1973) writes:

The idea of death, the fear of it, haunts the human animal like nothing else: it is the mainspring of human activity—activity designed to avoid death—to overcome it by denying it.

Whence is this universal horror of death if it is 'only natural'? The biblical authors confront the unnaturalness of death by speaking of Death as a power which holds a person in thrall. The Funeral Service itself says 'In the midst of life we are in death'. The reality and the finality of death are confronted directly.

In the understanding of biblical theology, death is described in uncomfortable language as a symbol of divine judgment. There is a negative aspect to death of which we cannot say, as God did of the perfection of creation, 'this is good'. Death has a negative and unnatural component. Yet it is an evil used by God as a sign of his judgment against *all* that is disordered and ungodly about life. Thus:

The man who fears death, even though he contrives to put a somewhat better face on it, is at least nearer to the truth than the man who does not fear it, or rather pretends that there is no reason why he should do so. Since it is the sign of the divine judgment of human sin and guilt, it is very much to be feared.   (Barth 1935, p. 589.

The Gospel accounts of the ministry of Jesus indicate how, when confronted with sickness, disorder, and death in others, 'he almost invariably shows himself a fighter'. For him, even sickness was not natural but was seen as an unnatural intrusion into the goodness of creation, to be confronted and resisted. Likewise with death: at the grave of his friend Lazarus, Jesus snorted with indignation and wept with grief (Coggan 1975).

Yet the supreme paradox, as well as the climax, of the Gospels is that Jesus himself dies. Jesus, God incarnate, himself suffers death as the judgment of God. The New Testament faith affirms that those who by faith are 'in him' are freed from experiencing this judgment. For the Christian, the 'sting' of death is drawn. He is no longer under this threat of divine judgment. The last enemy is overcome. Death, in the death of Christ, is declared to be God's enemy as well, and God:

> treats it as such by placing Himself at the side of man in the verdict there pronounced, and snatching man from its jaws by the death of Jesus for him. It remains for us as a sign of the divine judgement. We have no longer to suffer the judgement itself   (Barth 1935, p. 600.)

One focus of the New Testament is thus the death of Christ; but the New Testament says more. It says that the God who meets us in the death of Christ is 'for us', and the evidence is that God raised Christ from the dead. The resurrection is both the objective factual basis for the certainty of Christian faith, and the subjective assurance that faith in Christ is not faith in vain. Whereas, therefore, death means the end of our existence in time, it does not mean our extinction. The resurrection of Christ stands as a 'sure and certain hope' of *our* resurrection. This hope, though not removing the objective unnaturalness associated with death, enables us also to receive our death as a gift of divine love. Thus death in the New Testament is spoken of as 'falling asleep' in Christ, of 'setting sail for another shore', of departing to 'be with Christ which is far better'. For those for whom the sting of death is drawn, death becomes but one phase of natural life. It is the transition from personal life clothed in a physical body to personal life in a 'spiritual' body. We do not lose something at death to become disembodied spirits. We gain the enrichment and transformation of resurrection. Life can thus be enriched through suffering and death. Suffering itself can be redemptive and creative.

Christian faith, in a deeply real sense, therefore, is a faith which helps people to die; (and to some degree precisely because of this, it is a faith which helps people to live). The Christian pastor bears this understanding and interpreation of the meaning of death and of suffering. He seeks to make sense of the pain of loss to the dying person and the grieving family. He cannot do so either by denying the sharp reality of death, or by failing to help his people as far as possible to prepare for it. However, his Gospel points also to a God whose love is shown in his involvement in his people's vulnerability and pain. God is not 'untouched with the feeling of our infirmities'. He has 'borne our griefs and carried our sorrows'. He can take our anger, and share our need. The theology of the Cross shows how death and the depths of suffering can be redemptive and healing. Part of the task of pastoral care for those suffering with grief is to help them use their sufferings creatively and in a way which fosters growth. It is because the pastor (and this is true also for the doctor, and others offering care) has faced his own anxieties about his own death that he is able to give support and encouragement to those who grieve.

COPING WITH GRIEF

What do the 'representative' and 'reconciling' functions involve in the pastoral care of the dying and grieving? How is the pastor to help others take the reality of death seriously, and help them prepare for it?

The dying

The experience of grief is universal. It is a normal response to the loss of some significant person of object. Divorce, unemployment, the death of a pet, moving house, going abroad, the amputation of a limb are all examples of losses which can cause grief. For a dying person all his losses come together at the same time in the impending loss of his own life. He is also faced with the fundamentally different aspects of the loss of death, namely its finality.

Pastoral care of the dying person is primarily concerned with helping him come to terms with this impending loss. Our understanding of the emotional components of such grief has been considerably enhanced in recent years through the work of Dr Elizabeth Kubler-Ross. In the 1960s Dr Kubler-Ross established a seminar at the University of Chicago to consider the implications of terminal illness for the patients and for those involved in their care. Her accounts of the attitudes which surfaced during many conversations and interviews are recorded in her book *On death and dying* (1970). She indicates the following stages through which a patient may pass in coming to terms with his or her own death: Denial and Isolation; Anger; Bargaining; Depression; Acceptance, and Hope. There are many whose grief does not follow a prescribed pattern. Nevertheless, such 'stages' can help a pastor understand what is going on. Along with such emotional adjustments experienced in the process of coming to terms with one's own death, a patient will also, especially after an accident, or certain sorts of illness, find difficulty in coming to terms with a 'change of body image'. There is also the gnawing uncertainty of what will happen to the family left behind (Ainsworth-Smith and Speck 1982).

How does the pastor care for the dying person in the family? Ainsworth-Smith and Speck (1982) isolate four aspects to the pastoral task, which draw together threads we have touched on before. First, the pastor can help to *reconcile*: that is, re-establish broken relationships between man and God, and between man and man, and frequently within the patient himself. Secondly, he can help to *sustain*: the dying person needs support and sustenance if he or she is to endure and transcend what is happening to mind and body. Thirdly, he is there to *guide*: many people look to the clergy to guide them in what to do, in their understanding of what is happening to them, and of their faith. Fourthly, he can *enable growth* so that the dying person can, with the time that is available, use even the dying process as a time of healing.

In her book *Death and the family*, Lily Pincus (1976) makes reference to the strange reports of some patients near to the time of death who have come back briefly into consciousness and reported experiencing 'another world'. She quotes the view of a Roman Catholic priest who does not pretend to understand such reports, but wisely adds:

All I know is that this phenomenon places a great responsibility on the people around the dying patient, not to interfere through drugs, thoughlessness or impatience with what may well be his most important experience, and may give meaning to his dying.

Whatever the status of the reports of paranormal experiences, this priest's caution serves as a reminder how important a person's experience of dying can be. Many readers have been helped by the story of a young family doctor who died of cancer at the age of 37, who called his little book *Dying: the greatest adventure of my life*, (Casson 1980).

Within these four aims, the pastoral task can involve various practical 'means of grace' alongside the ongoing giving of time, support and comfort, and meaning. For some people these will involve prayer, meditation and Bible reading; for some sacramental ministry, sometimes called Extreme Unction. However for all, it is the quality of the pastoral relationship that is most important. Not all clergy are particularly good at this sort of ministry. As Dr Kubler-Ross (1970) says:

What amazed me was the number of clergy who felt quite comfortable using a prayer book or a chapter out of the Bible as the sole communication between them and the patients, thus avoiding listening to their needs and being exposed to questions they might be unable or unwilling to answer.

Even for those who are alert to the need for personal relationship, the task is not easy. The clergyman carries with him a series of complex expectancies. He is expected to be able to 'answer for God'. Often he is the bearer of the sick person's anger against God (or against the doctor, or the hospital). The fact that the pastor can often only share the pain without an 'answer' sometimes makes the care of the dying one of the most demanding of his pastoral tasks.

The bereaved

There is a growing literature concerned with the processes of grief and mourning, much of it written to help society re-learn that death is an inescapable part of life, and that freer discussion of the processes of grieving might contribute to a more accepting attitude to mourning. Such literature helps those involved as carers both to understand the nature and phases of 'normal' grief, and to be aware of abnormal grieving which may require specialist help.

Normal grief

Apart from Freud's early paper on mourning (1917), the first study to concentrate seriously on the management of acute grief as a definite syndrome with psychological and somatic symptomatology, was that of Erich Lindemann. In 1944 he published a paper, which argued that a clearly defined grief syndrome may appear immediately after a crisis, or may be delayed, or even sometimes be apparently absent. In place of the typical syndrome there may sometimes be distortions and abnormalities, but by the use of appropriate techniques, distorted pictures can be transformed back into 'normal' grief. Lindemann, with Freud, used the concept of 'grief work'. By that he meant that grieving is a process of coping which involves working at emancipation from bondage to the loss of the deceased, re-adjustment to the environment in which the deceased is missing, and the formation of new relationships. Since Lindemann's classic work, which although clear was not, by modern standards, a well-conducted study (having no control group), others have made important contributions to our understanding of the processes of grief. The work of Elizabeth Kubler-Ross with the dying has already been mentioned. Dr Colin Murray Parkes' studies of grief in adult life, published in 1972, cover similar ground on the basis of over 10 years work with bereaved people. From within the psychoanalytic tradition Lily Pincus published her partly theoretical and partly anecdotal book *Death and the family* in 1976, and in 1977 Yorick Spiegel wrote *The grief process*. Spiegel's work is both practical and pastoral, bringing together psychotherapy, sociology, and theology in a very full interdisciplinary study.

Loss through bereavement is a crisis in which all a person's previous equilibrium is upset. The normal responses are inadequate. The behaviour of bereaved people may become very unpredictable, and lead them to a sense of shame for the embarrassment they believe they cause. There can be a real loss of the 'self'. In this crisis, various so-called 'phases' of grief are often evident. The processes are now well documented, and one summary is found in Table 8.1 which is taken from Ainsworth-Smith and Speck's book *Letting go* (1982). C. M. Parkes' work (1972) follows a similar

Table 8.1. 'Normal' patterns of bereavement behaviour

	Denial	Developing awareness	Resolution
	Death of spouse up to 2 weeks	2 weeks–2 years	2–5 years
Physical reactions	Shock	Loss of vitality. Physical symptoms of stress. Irrational behaviour—often coming in waves lasting 20–60 min Psychosomatic illness, often parallels symptoms of deceased. (May not be reversed)	
Emotional	Numbness Cotton wool feeling Denial	Outbursts of grief (pining, crying, exhaustion) Depression or Sadness Anger—against deceased, medicine, God ('why') Loss of confidence and self-approval Guilt ('if only') Loneliness—especially in older bereaved Idealizing of the deceased	'Resolution' 1. The resolve that one will cope 2. Sense of detachment allowing freedom of action 3. Feeling it is now alright to enjoy social contacts, etc.
External factors affecting behaviour	Circumstances of death and funeral arrangements Family Religious beliefs and culture	Financial loss or gain Loss of status Anniversaries Society's disapproval of overt emotion and avoidance of death	Acceptance of new status by society. Role of organizations such as: Cruse Society for Compassionate Friends

NB Grief work may commence prior to the death of the patient.
From Ainsworth-Smith and Speck (1982).

progression, but isolates four main phases: a phase of numbness, shock, and partial disregard of the reality of the loss; a phase of yearning, with an urge to recover the lost object; a phase of disorganization, despair, and gradual coming to terms with the reality of the loss; a phase of reorganization and resolution. Though normal grief usually includes such phases, there is, of course, no universal pastoral technique. As Ainsworth-Smith and Speck (1982) say:

Grief is a very complex process and so it is not surprising, therefore, that for some it continues for a long time, or is never really completed, whilst for others it seems to progress gradually without the need for any sort of intervention except for a sensitive listening ear.

It is important to stress that these so-called phases often overlap and are sometimes repeated in different ways in different contexts. C. S. Lewis's (1961) masterly personal description of his own bereavement illustrates this:

Tonight all the hells of young grief have opened again; the mad words, the bitter resentment, the fluttering in the stomach, the nightmare unreality, the wallowed-in tears. For in grief nothing 'stays put'. One keeps on emerging from a phase, but it always recurs. Round and round. Everything repeats. Am I going in circles, or dare I hope I am on a spiral? But if a spiral, am I going up or down it?

At each phase, the pastor can facilitate grief work in two ways: by being aware of what is happening to the person, and sometimes interpreting it to them; and also by 'being there' as a resource and point of reference while the whole of person's previous assumptive world is being challenged and changed. It is important to work at the bereaved's own pace, allowing time for reminiscence, allowing space for anger. Grief is not to be rushed, nor denied.

Grief must often be understood and managed as a family experience. Loss through bereavement, especially loss of a marriage partner, is a major change not only in the bereaved person's 'inner world', but also in all the external relationships of which he or she is a part. How people experience and handle loss will be affected by their own emotional histories and often by the extent to which their early learning experiences have affected their ability to cope with loss. If there are previous unresolved losses in a person's life, bereavement may be a time when these earlier pains resurface. John Bowlby (1974) stresses how the experiences of 'attachment and loss' in early childhood, and the need for the growing child to cope with 'separation anxiety', are the main keys to understanding the processes of mourning. Earlier, Melanie Klein (1940) had written:

The pain experienced in the slow process of testing reality in the work of mourning seems to be partly due to the necessity, not only to renew the links to the external world and thus continuously re-experience the loss, but at the same time, and by means of this, to rebuild with anguish the inner world, which is felt to be in danger of deteriorating and collapsing.

To the pastors caring for the family, in which each person is experiencing their own grief, as well as sharing in the grief of each other, Parkes (1964) makes the following suggestions. First, an awareness that much pain can be prevented if a person about to be bereaved can be encouraged to express some grief in anticipation. Secondly, a willingness to share the grief, but not to force it. Thirdly, a realization that the pastor cannot give the bereaved person what they really want, that is, their loved one back again. Fourthly, the mobilization of wider family and friends who can do a great deal to cushion the blow. At some stage, it may be appropriate for the pastor to bring together a group of bereaved people in a self-support group. Fifthly, eventually the pastor may be able to help the grieving person set limits to their grief, and mobilize them into taking responsible steps towards re-adjustment. Finally, the pastor needs to be constantly alert to the possibilities that grief may become pathological, and other help may be needed.

Grieving children can often best be helped by helping the bereaved parent. Much of a child's grief may be a reflection of the parent's. If the adult can be encouraged to express feelings, and be advised that it is not harmful for the child to do likewise, both parent and child can be helped. As Lily Pincus (1976) writes: 'Human beings need to mourn in response to loss, and if they are denied this, they will suffer psychologically or physically or both'.

Abnormal grief

At each phase of grief, things can go wrong. After the initial shock and numbness, when feelings begin to emerge they are often expressions of protest, often tears. These appropriate expressions may sometimes be suppressed, and the true feelings denied. If so, various abnormal reactions may follow. For some there can be a 'superspirituality', based on the idea that to acknowledge grief must be a sign of unbelief. There may be a tendency to overactivity which avoids facing the reality of the death. Death may be denied by 'mummifying' the deceased's room or belongings, or by fantasizing idealized pictures of the deceased. There may in some be a very strong temptation to 'contact' the deceased through spiritualism. Anger which is not acknowledged may be projected on to the pastor, the doctor or the hospital. The normal depression associated with the phase of yearning or despair may develop into a chronic depressive illness associated with overwhelming feelings of guilt. The later phase of acceptance, of gradually coming to terms with the loss may be diverted by withdrawal from friends and family. The bereaved can become a recluse. Alternatively, the grieving person can become over-dependent on others and develop an irresponsible helplessness. If any of these abnormal reactions become chronic, resolution may not be reached without skilled intervention, and the bereaved will stay feeling alone and in the dark, instead of gradually emerging into the light.

The pastor needs to try to understand what is going on in the bereaved person and in the family, and to encourage referral for medical and sometime psychiatric care if the grief becomes pathological. He must be alert to the mechanisms of defence and denial which can be very strong. He may be one of those able to create possibilities of communication between the grieving person and the painful outer world.

The pastor's task is to help the grieving person overcome the tendencies to build abnormal defences against the pain of the loss, and open them to the resources which will help towards resolution. If the grieving person is holding persistent guilt or unforgiving feelings, the pastor may be the one person through whom the possibilities of forgiveness, reparation, and restitution can be experienced.

Abnormal grief may well need specialist help. However, it must not be assumed that all grief is pathological. To quote Lily Pincus (1976):

It would be fatal . . . to give the impression that bereavement *as such* with all its agonies and confusions, all its pain and bewilderment, needs therapeutic intervention. What it needs is the recognition that grief is the normal response to the loss of a loved person, and that it is of fundamental importance to work through the mourning process and for it to be completed without harmful interference or repression.

A pastor working within a theological framework such as outlined has a basis for understanding the fear and rejection of death as, in one sense, an 'unnatural enemy', and also for accepting and facilitating the processes of dying and grieving as, in another sense, natural and normal. His faith in God's grace and in the transformation of resurrection give him confidence in helping others face the reality of death, and more adequately to prepare for it.

THE PLACE OF RITUAL IN GRIEVING

We turn now to the pastor's ritual function. In his book *Rites of passage* (1960), Arnold Van Gennep gave an account of the ways in which social groups, whether secular or religious, tend to develop various rituals to help individuals cope with life crises and transitions. A ritual helps a person to *interpret* the changes that are happening in his life. It helps to focus the *choices* which are open to him, and helps him to make a decision. The ritual helps him to *make the move* from one phase of life to another.

Funerals can exercise these functions for the bereaved, and the pastor's role at the funeral involves these three aspects. The community of faith, which the pastor represents, can act as a support and help in these tasks of interpretation, choosing, and 'making the move' which a death in the family demands.

For the person of faith, the setting of the death rituals in the context of a theological understanding of reality, helps give an interpretation to the death and the loss. Christian faith with its understanding of resurrection of life, helps the bereaved face the loss of death, and turn the pain of bereavement into a sense of hope and confidence. The resources of the community of faith, resources of the grace of God, and the support of friends, help the bereaved person in the choice whether the death of the loved one will for ever remain an open wound, or whether there will be creative movement towards building a new life. The move from being John the husband to John the widower can be helped by the physical, temporal, social event of the funeral, marking for him and for his society the ending of one phase of his life and the beginning of another.

Van Gennep (1960) separates out three sorts of ritual: rites of *separation*, such as the Bar Mitzvah of a Jewish boy, or a coming of age ceremony; rites of *transition*, such as a wedding and honeymoon; rites of *reincorporation* or reunion, such as the dedication of a new home. A funeral service, together with the pastoral preparation beforehand, and often the family gathering afterwards, has aspects of all three. There is the enactment of the *separation* between the grieving family and the one who has died, seen in the lowering of the coffin into the grave, or symbolized by the drawing of a curtain at the crematorium. This helps the bereaved to face the reality of death. It also serves to remind the living to face their own eventual death. There is *transition* in the prayers commending the loved one to God's merciful keeping: a ritual handing over of some of the pain of separation to God. And there is *reincorporation* in the commitment of the mourners to God's loving care and protection, and the presence of a caring fellowship extending support. The funeral, then, can be an important part of the grief process. It provides a formal and ritual context in which the strong emotions of grief can be appropriately and publicly acknowledged, and in which symbolically the bereaved can be helped in the processes of 'letting go'. Along with the ritual acting out of grief emotions, there is in a Christian funeral also the opportunity to set these in the context of God's grace. The pastor stands for the presence of the Christian community, assuring the bereaved person that they are not alone.

The value of the funeral ritual can be reinforced through careful subsequent pastoral contract with the bereaved family. Other rituals act as reinforcers, such as the visiting of the 'focus' of the grave of 'place of memory'. Partly in the crucially important lonely weeks immediately after the funeral, and partly also at significant times like the first anniversary, the pastoral function is that of support in the continuing grief work ritually focused in the funeral.

It is interesting that the lack of ritual mourning may contribute to an inadequate resolution of grief; especially in those parts of our society where such religious rituals are not held to be significant, there is a noticeable increase in the number of counselling agencies offering help to the bereaved (Pincus 1976).

LOSS AND GROWTH

The theology of the Cross indicated that suffering can be redemptive and creative. Several Christian writers have recently made this their theme. To take two examples: first, in *Creative suffering* (1982), the Swiss doctor Paul Tournier suggests that much of the creativity in art, science, and medicine is linked to a driving force of suffering behind it. What we suffer, he believes, can be made part of our processes of maturing and growing. Secondly, Dr Martin Israel also explores this theme in *The pain that heals* (1981), writing that: 'it is one of the fundamental contributions of pain to make people wake up to a deeper level of existence'. Both writers indicate how the experiences of loss can be opportunities for personal growth.

This is a theme not limited to theological writers. The psychoanalyst Klein (1959), for example, links the capacity for creativity to what she calls the Depressive Position (a painful phase of emotional development and painful pattern of emotional response.) Erik Erikson's discussion of personal identity also shows how crisis phases of emotional development are all crucial periods both of increased vulnerability and of heightened potential. It is the successful negotiation of the critical phases of life which leads to maturity and growth Erikson (1968).

One of the important tasks for the pastor, therefore, is to seek to help the dying and the grieving understand and use their different experiences of loss in ways that are creative. For the Christian, suffering can be understood in some sense as 'sharing in' the redemptive sufferings of God in Christ. As St. Paul writes:

> Blessed be the God and Father of our Lord Jesus Christ, the Father of mercies and God of all comfort, who comforts us in all our affliction, so that we may be able to comfort those who are in any affliction, with the comfort with which we ourselves are comforted by God. For as we share abundantly in Christ's sufferings, so through Christ we share abundantly in comfort too. (2 Cor.1:3–5)

It is of interest that the word translated 'comfort' has a range of meanings from 'stand alongside', 'console', 'sympathize with', 'entreat', 'warn', 'exhort', 'support' to 'strengthen'. All of these, at different times, may be part of the pastor's task as he seeks to encourage those suffering loss to find, in that experience, something of the grace of God by which they can be helped to grow.

REFERENCES

Ainsworth-Smith, I. and Speck, P. (1982). *Letting go*.SPCK, London.
Argyle, M. and Beit-Hallahmi, B. (1975). *The social psychology of religion*. Routledge and Kegan-Paul, London.

Barth, K. (1935). *Church dogmatics*. Vol. 111/2. Clark, Edinburgh.
Becker, E. (1973). *The denial of death*. Macmillan, London and New York.
Bowlby, J. (1974). *Attachment and loss*. Hogarth, London.
Campbell, A. (1981). *Rediscovering pastoral care*. Darton, Longman and Todd, London.
Casson, J. (1980). *Dying: the greatest adventure of my life*. The Christian Medical Fellowship, London.
Coggan, F. D. (1975). *Convictions*. Hodder and Stoughton, London.
Erikson, E. (1968). *Identity: youth and crisis*. Faber, London.
Freud, S. (1917). Mourning and melancholia. In: *Collected Papers* Vol. 4 (Freud, S. 1953). Hogarth, London.
Van Gennep, A. (1960). *Rites of passage*. Univ. of Chicago.
Israel, M. (1981). *The pain that heals*. Hodder and Stoughton, London.
Klein, M. (1940). Mourning and its relation to manic depressive states. *Int. J. Psycho Anal.* **21**, 125–53.
—— (1975). Our Adult world and its roots in infancy. In: *Envy and Gratitude*. Hogarth, London.
Kubler-Ross, E. (1970). *On death and dying*. Tavistock, London.
Lewis, C. S. (1961). *A grief observed*. Faber, London.
Lindemann, E. (1944). The symptomatology and management of acute grief. *American Journal of Psychiatry* September, 7f.
Moberg, D. O. (1973). Religiosity in old age. In: *Psychology and religion* (L. Brown (ed.), Penguin, Harmondsworth.
Parkes, C. M. (1964). *Contact*. **12**, p. 300.
—— (1972). *Bereavement*. Penguin, Harmondsworth.
Pincus, L. (1976). *Death and the family*. Faber, London.
Spiegel, Y. (1977). *The grief process*. SCM, London.
Tournier, P. (1982). *Creative suffering*. SCM, London.

FURTHER READING

Klein, M. (1937). *Love, hate and reparation*. Hogarth, London.
Thielicke, H. (1983). *Living with death* (Eerdmans), Grand Rapids.

We shall not cease from exploration
And the end of all our exploring
Will be to arrive where we started
And know the place for the first time.
Through the unknown, remembered gate
When the last of earth left to discover
Is that which was the beginning;
At the source of the longest river
The voice of the hidden waterfall
And the children in the apple-tree
Not known, because not looked for
But heard, half-heard, in the stillness
Between two waves of the sea.
Quick now, here, now, always—
A condition of complete simplicity
(Costing not less than everything)
And all shall be well and
All manner of thing shall be well
When the tongues of flame are in-folded
Into the crowned knot of fire
And the fire and the rose are one.

T. S. Eliot
From *Four Quartets*

Index

adolescents, understanding of dying process in 86–7
age, understanding of dying process and 86–7
amitriptyline 48
analgesics 41, 43–9
  additional medication 47
  administration by relatives 76–7
  choice of 44, 45–7, 48
  mixtures 48–9
  route of administration 43–4, 46
  side-effects 49
  timing of dose 43, 44
  see also specific agents
animal behaviour and attitudes to death 5–6
anorexia 52–3, 71–2
antibiotics 48, 102–3
antiemetics 36, 47, 49–50, 52, 71
anxiety
  in the bereaved 9–11, 75
  in patients 41, 42, 47, 59–60
arthralgia, metastatic 57
Asilone 48, 53, 54
aspirin 45, 48, 49

back pain 43, 67
baclofen 48
Bandor pads 68
Bath District Health Authority 21–2, 26
beds, loan of hospital 67
bedsores, prevention of 66–7
belladonna alkaloids, rectal 48
bereavement
  care 9–11, 128, 139–43
  growth from 145
  see also grief
birth at home 8
body splints 67
bone pain 41, 43, 48
bowels
  management of 69–71
  obstruction of 37, 50–2
buprenorphine 46

cancer
  corticosteroids 56–7

financial help 79
nausea and vomiting 49–50, 51
pain in 39, 40, 48
rehabilitation 104
candidiasis 65–6
carbamazepine 48
cerebral oedema 57
cerebral tumours
  children 113–15, 120
  treatment 57, 103
chaplains, hospital and hospice 108
children
  dying at home 120
  grieving 142
  a hospice for, see Helen House, Oxford
  profoundly handicapped 121
  understanding of dying process 86
chlormethiazole 60
chlorpromazine 48, 50, 52, 60
Christian faith, attitudes to death and 87–8, 136–7, 144
Christian theology
  death and 134–7
  hospices and 107–8
  on loss and growth 145
Citizen's Advice Bureau 80
cocaine 48, 60
codeine 45, 52
colostomies 70–1, 76
colostomy bags 67, 68, 71
communication 30–1, 83–94
  definition 83
  doctor–patient, see doctor–patient
  communication within families 63, 74, 93–4
community-based services 20–1, 28–30;
  see also home care services
community (district) nurses 33, 78, 79, 81
Community Nursing Division 26, 28
compression pumps for lymphoedema 55–6, 73
confusional states 58–60, 73–4
constipation 47, 69
consultation, doctor–patient 14–15, 83, 84–6
Continuing Care Units (hospices), NHS 97, 98, 99
corticosteroids 48, 52, 56–7, 103
Council of Voluntary Services 80

creativity, loss and 145
Cruse 11
cyclizine 50, 51, 52, 53
cystic fibrosis, a case history 122–3

day care facilities 22, 98
death
  animal behaviour and 5–6
  Christian theology and 87–8, 134–7, 144
  contemporary attitudes to 6–11, 86–9
  fear of 5–6, 42, 87, 89
  history of attitudes to 4–5
  medicalization of 5–6
  place of 1, 2, 16–17, 110
denial 63–4, 134–5
Department of Health and Social Security (DHSS) 78–9
depression 37, 41, 47, 142
dexamethasone 52, 57
  cerebral tumours 48, 57, 60, 103
  nerve compression 42–3, 48, 57
dexamphetamine 60
dextromoramide 46
dextropropoxyphene 45
diamorphine 46, 47
diazepam 48, 60, 69
diphenoxylate 52
dipipanone 46
discharging lesions, care of 67–8
district (community) nurses 33, 78, 79, 81
doctor–patient communication 83, 84–6, 106, 108
  model of 84–5
  patient satisfaction with 83
  problems in 89–93
doctors
  communication with families 83, 93
  home care teams 26–7
  training 16, 89
  understanding of the dying process 88–9
  see also consultation, doctor–patient; general practitioner
docusate (Dioctyl) 52
domiciliary care services 20–1, 22, 28–30; see also home care services
domperidone 51
Dorothy House Foundation 21–6
  administration 26
  advisory committee 26
  Assessment Unit 22
  day care 22
  domiciliary service 22
  education programme 23
  evaluation of the service 23
  statistical review 24–5
  volunteers 22–3
drug treatment 36–8, 98
  administration by relatives 76–7
  appropriate 102–3
  in bereavement 11
  timing 36–7, 43, 44
  see also analgesics; *specific agents*
dysphagia 72
dyspnoea 72–3

effleurage 55
elderly
  characteristics of population 2–4
  understanding of dying process 86–7
Eliot, T. S., quoted 147
emollient creams 36, 67
emotional care
  children and their families 125–8
  patients 63–5, 100
  of relatives and close friends 74–6
enemas 52, 69–70
environment, communication and 88
equipment and aids, free loan of 81
Eusol and liquid paraffin packs 88

faeces
  impaction 69–70
  manual removal 69, 70
families
  communication within 63, 74, 93–4
  financial help 78–9
  pastoral care 131–45
  practical advice and information 78–81
  value of home care teams 32–3
  see also bereavement; parents; relatives
Fanconi's anaemia, a case history 123–4
fear of death 5–6, 42, 87, 89
financial help for families 78–9
'Fish' schemes 80
fistulae 70
Flowpulse intermittent compression pump 55
flurbiprofen 48
food, appropriate 53, 71, 72
Four Quartets by T. S. Eliot, quoted 147
funerals 4, 131, 143–5
fungating tumours 68–9, 76

gastric distension pain 48, 53–4
Gaviscon 54
general practitioner 13–16, 79
  access to hospital beds 12, 13
  home care services and 11, 28–9, 30–3, 98
  hospices and 26–7, 109–10
  training 16
  see also doctors; consultation, doctor–patient; primary care teams

Index 151

'Good Neighbour' schemes 80
grief 75, 137–43
   abnormal 9, 142–3
   Christian theological approach 134–7
   of the dying 137–8
   normal 9–11, 139–42
   role of ritual in 143–5
   see also bereavement

hallucinations 58, 59, 60
haloperidol 50, 51, 52, 60
handicapped children, care of 121
health visitors 78, 79–80, 81
Helen House, Oxford 8, 113–29
   administration and finance 118–19
   the building 115–17
   case histories 122–5
   emotional and spiritual care 125–8
   Helen's history 113–15
   home care 118
   liaison with other agencies and families 118–19
   pattern of visits 121–2
   practical care 129
   referrals 122
   selection of children 120–1
   staff support 118
   the team 117
hepatomegaly 53
home, births at 8
home care services 11–13, 19–34
   demand for 19–20
   hospice-based 11, 20, 21, 26–7, 97–8, 118
   hospital-based 11, 20, 21, 27–8
   see also nursing care at home
home care teams 12, 20–1, 62
   establishing 33
   general practitioners and 30–3
   primary care team and 26–30
home helps 80
hope, maintenance of 90, 105–6
hospices 7–8, 96–111
   appropriate treatment 100–3
   bereavement care 11
   for children, see Helen House, Oxford
   definition 119
   evaluation of care 99–100
   goals of 96
   home care services 11, 20, 21, 26–7, 97–8, 118
   hope 105–6
   need for 19, 20, 109–10
   professional friendship 106
   rehabilitation 104–5
   team-work 108–9
   types of provision 97–9

'whole-person care' 106–8
hospitals
   admission to 1, 2–4, 12, 13, 32
   death in 6–7
   general practitioner 12
   home care services based in 11, 20, 21, 27–8
   symptom control teams 99
hospital support teams 12, 20, 21, 27–8

ileostomies 70–1
immobilization to relieve pain 43
insomnia, treatment of 9–11, 49
intracranial pressure, raised 48, 57

Kubler-Ross, Dr Elizabeth 137, 138

laundry services 81
levorphanol 46
lymphoedema, management of 48, 54–6, 73

Macmillan Homes or Units 97
Macmillan nurses 11, 12, 21
   role of 19–20, 79, 97–8, 99
   see also nurses, specialist domiciliary
Marie Curie Foundation 12, 21
Marie Curie Homes 97, 98, 99
Marie Curie nurses 21, 80
meals-on-wheels service 81
medical aids and equipment, loan of 81
medicine, high technology 5–6
methadone 37, 46
metoclopramide 48, 49–50, 51, 53
metronidazole 48
ministers of religion 81; see also pastoral care
morphine
   adjunctive drugs 48–9
   recommendations for use 36–7, 46, 47, 48, 52
   side effect 47, 49
mouth care 65–6
muscle spasm pain 48

naproxen 48
naso-gastric feeding 72
National Health Service (NHS)
   Continuing Care Units (hospices) 97, 98, 99
   home care services 12, 13
National Society for cancer Relief (NSCR) 11, 19, 21, 22, 79, 97

nausea, treatment of 49–50, 51
nerve compression pain 42–3, 48, 57
night nurses 80, 98
night-sitters 12, 80
non-Hodgkin's lymphoma, a case history 124–5
non-steroidal anti-inflammatory drugs 45
nurses 94
  community (district) 33, 78, 79, 81
  Macmillan, see Macmillan nurses
  Marie Curie 21, 80
  night 80, 98
  specialist domiciliary 27, 28–30, 31–2;
    see also Macmillan nurses
nursing auxillaries 80
nursing care at home 62–82
  emotional support 63–5
  general philosophy 62
  individualized 62–3
  physical aspects 65–74
  practical advice and information 78–81
  relatives and close friends 74–8
nursing homes 12, 98–9

occupational therapists, domiciliary 81
odours, control of 68
oesophagitis 54
orphenadrine 50
oxycodone 46

pain
  assessment 15, 39–41
  causes 39, 40
  control 16, 38–49, 76–7, 100
  treatment modalities 41–3
  see also analgesics
papaveretum 46
paracetamol 45
paraplegic patients, bowel movements in 70
parents
  emotional and spiritual care 125–8
  facilities for 115, 117, 121
Parkes, C. M. 9, 139–41
pastoral care 108, 131–45
  the bereaved 139–43
  the dying 137–8
  loss and growth 145
  ritual 143–5
patient participation groups 8
patients
  emotional care 63–5, 100
  individualized care 62–3, 106–8
  needs of 109
  overprotection 77–8
  pastoral care 137–8

understanding of dying process 86–8
  see also doctor–patient communication
pentazocine 46
pethidine 44, 46
phenazocine 46
phenothiazines 48, 50
physiotherapists, domiciliary 81
Pincus. L. 134, 138, 139, 142, 143
prednisolone 48, 52, 57
pressure area care 66–7
primary care teams 94, 99
  home care teams and 19–20, 26–30
prochlorperazine 50, 51
promazine 60
pruritus, relief of 36
psychiatrist, child 118

rectal tenesmoid pain 48
recto-vaginal fistula 68, 70
recto-vesical fistula 70
Red Cross, loans of equipment from 81
rehabilitation 77, 104–5
relatives
  communication with doctors 83, 93
  emotional care 74–6, 100, 125–8
  looking after the elderly 2–4
  overprotection by 77–8
  teaching nursing skills to 76–7
  see also bereavement; families; parents
religious beliefs, attitudes to death and 87–8, 131; see also Christian faith
respite care 12, 113, 119, 121
restlessness 73
ritual mourning 131, 143–5

St. Christopher's Hospice, London 7–8, 11, 20, 96, 97, 119
St. Joseph's Hospice, Hackney 11, 97, 119
Samaritans 11
Saunders, Dame Cicely 7–8, 96, 107–8, 119
self-help groups 8, 11, 142
siblings of dying children 121, 127
skin care 36, 67–8, 71
social environment, attitudes to death and 88
social workers 81, 118
Society for Compassionate Friends 11
spinal lesions, care of 67
spiritual care 107–8, 125–8
'squashed stomach syndrome' 53–4
staff, psychological costs to 118
stocking-bandage, shaped elastic 55
stoma care 70–1
Sue Ryder Foundation 12

Sue Ryder Homes 97, 98, 99
suicidal thoughts 9, 11, 90
suppositories 46, 47, 69, 70, 76
symptom control 28–9, 35–60, 102
   teams 99
   see also treatment, appropriate; *specific symptoms*, e.g. pain; vomiting

terminal illness, concept of 119
theological approach to death 134–7; *see also* Christian theology
thioridazine 60
thrush, oral 65–6
tranquillizers 11, 42, 73

treatment, appropriate 36–8, 100–3; *see also* drug treatment; symptom control
Tubigrip elastic stocking-bandage 55

ulcers, malignant 48, 68–9, 76

valproate 48
voluntary organizations 80
volunteers 22–3, 99
vomiting
   obstructive 37, 50–2
   treatment of 49–50, 51